Muslim Citizens of the Globalized World:

Contributions of the Gülen Movement

Edited by

Robert A. Hunt
Yüksel A. Aslandoğan

Published by The Light, Inc & IID Press

26 Worlds Fair Dr Unit C

Somerset, NJ, 08873, USA

www.thelightpublishing.com

contact@thelightinc.com

Edited by

Robert A. Hunt

Yüksel A. Aslandoğan

Designed by

Aytekin Aydoğdu

Helix Design & Production, LLC

www.helixpro.com

Library of Congress Cataloging-in-Publication Data
Muslim citizens of the globalized world : contributions of the Gülen
movement / edited by Robert A. Hunt, Yüksel A. Aslandoğan.
1st ed.
p. cm.
Includes bibliographical references and index.
ISBN 1-59784-073-4 (pbk.)
1. Gülen, Fethullah. 2. Islam—20th century. 3. Islam—21st century.
4. Globalization—Religious aspects—Islam. 5. Islam and world politics.
I. Hunt, Robert A. II. Aslandoğan, Yüksel A.
BP161.3.M849 2007
297.092—dc22

2006031134

Printed and bound

By Victor Graphics, Inc.

Baltimore, MD

September 2006

Contents

Preface

This volume brings together essays exploring the response and contributions of Muslims in general and Turkish Muslims in particular to the waves of democratization, scientific revolution, changing gender roles, and religious diversity in an increasingly globalized world. The book explores the thought of Fethullah Gülen, Turkish Muslim scholar, author, and education activist, known by some as "a modern-day Rumi," and his impact on the millions of participants in a social phenomenon called the Gülen movement. Originating in Turkey but becoming increasingly transnational, the movement represents novel approaches to the synthesis of faith and reason, peaceful co-existence in liberal democracies with religious diversity, education and spirituality.

The essay by Hendrick entitled "Transnational Muslim Social Movements and the Movement of Fethullah Gülen, A Comparative Approach" analyzes transnational Muslim social movements starting with the early Muslim community of the time of Prophet Muhammad[1] and seeks to

---

[1] Peace and blessings of God be upon him. In the rest of the book this phrase of reverence will not be repeated and will be assumed for the Muslim contributors.

show how the Gülen movement fits in the broader world of Muslim social movements.

Aslandoğan and Çetin's essay on the educational philosophy and activism of Gülen considers the various dimensions of a comprehensive approach to private secular education that aims to educate responsible citizens and empathetic human beings who are open to science and rationality, as well as the moral dimension of being human.

Jill Irvine's essay, which is based on a field study, explores Gülen movement activities in Germany and how the movement is contributing to the integration of people of Turkish origin into German society.

Paul Weller's essay explores the thought of Fethullah Gülen on religion, globalization, and dialogue. He analyzes Gülen's response to modernity as one between Herodian compromise and Zealot reaction using the perspectives of the British historian Arnold Toynbee, an extremely controversial writer from the Turkish point of view.

Ali Bulaç discusses Gülen as a Muslim scholar with an intellectual dimension and a representative of what he calls Civil Islam, as opposed to State Islam. He sees many elements of the Islamic *'ulama* tradition in Gülen, including the legitimacy and credibility coming from civil support. Bulaç sees Turkish modernization as a history of tension between people of faith and the state society. In Gülen's approach to issues such as the state, politics, and governance, Bulaç finds an opening for a dialogue between Civil Islam and State society.

Leonid Sykiainen discusses various perspectives on the relationship of democracy with Islam. He positions Gülen with those scholars who point to the flexibilities in Islamic political theory and its compatibility with democratic principles. Sykiainen underlines Gülen's stance against the domination of a religious clergy and his belief that secular and religious values and ideas can live peacefully side by side in the same society. The augmentation of the principles of consultation, equality, and justice with new ones such as tolerance, dialogue, positive activism, education, and cooperation against common concerns is a significant contribution of Gülen as a thinker in Sykiainen's perspective.

Albayrak's article considers the use of violence for political ends from an Islamic perspective. He examines the views of violence and terror in major Islamic texts and the notion of *jihad* in Islam. He discusses the fallacies in false justifications of war in the modern world, including suicide attacks. Finally, he outlines the positive role of dialogue and love of humanity as expressed in Gülen's thought and activism as providing a basis for overcoming the global calamity of terror.

Stephenson's essay provides evidence about the perspectives of women participants in the Gülen movement on social issues as demonstrated by their daily practices. Through qualitative research on the life histories of Turkish women living in the Houston area who are inspired by Fethullah Gülen's teachings, she shows some of the ways they make major life decisions.

Andrea traces Gülen's views on women, their rights and roles, starting with his gloss on the letters of Lady Mary Wortley Montagu. The wife of a British ambassador to the Ottoman Empire in the eighteenth century, Lady Montagu made many interesting observations on the rights and roles of Ottoman women and carried her observations back to her native country as a basis for her efforts to gain greater rights for women there. Andrea's analysis aims at correcting Western discourses on women's rights and roles in Islam, including mainstream Western feminist discourses, while challenging Muslim communities on customs that may have curtailed the full expression of women's rights according to the Qur'an and the prophetic example.

Gökçek positions Gülen's understanding of Islamic spirituality as firmly based on the Qur'an and the Sunna. He sees Gülen's understanding as exemplified in the second generation of Sufi masters, a generation marked by the presence of concepts and practices aimed at the purification of the heart without the traits of the Sufi orders as they emerged during the later centuries. In Gülen's understanding of Islamic spirituality Gökçek finds an approach that can re-awaken the larger world of Muslim communities to the rich spiritual dynamics of their faith.

The Graduate Program in Religious Studies at Southern Methodist University and the Boniuk Center for the Study and Advancement of Religious Tolerance both helped make this project possible by co-hosting conferences on the Gülen movement in Houston (November 2005) and Dallas (March 2006) respectively. The essays in this book are based on papers presented at these conferences.

We would like to thank Kudbettin Aksoy for his help, Hakan Yeşilova for his translations of Ali Bulaç's essay, and Ruth Woodhall of The Light Inc. for her support in preparing the manuscript.

Yüksel A. Aslandoğan

Contributors

Robert A. Hunt was born in Dallas, Texas, in 1955. He majored in history at the University of Texas in Austin. After completing a master's degree in theology at Perkins School of Theology (SMU), he served the Bethany United Methodist Church in Austin, Texas. In 1985, he and his wife Lillian moved to Kuala Lumpur, where they taught at the Theology Seminary, Malaysia. From 1993 to 1997, he taught at Trinity Theological College in Singapore. From 1997 to 2004, he was pastor of the English-speaking United Methodist Church of Vienna, and an adjunct professor at Webster University in Vienna. Dr. Hunt is presently Director of Global Theological Education at the Perkins School of Theology, Southern Methodist University.

Yüksel A. Aslandoğan is an adjunct faculty member at Prairie View A&M University and Vice President (Academic Programs) at the Institute of Interfaith Dialog in Houston, Texas. He is an author and an editorial board member for *The Fountain* magazine and has translated and compiled scientific articles for a popular scientific–spiritual magazine in Turkey since 1986. He has published articles and given seminars on topics including the relationship of science and religion, Islamic spirituality, comparative analysis of theories of learning and the prophetic tradition, and common cultural values among the world's major religions.

Muhammed Çetin is a visiting scholar at the Religious Studies Department of the University of Houston. He was a visiting scholar at the Sociology Department of UT Austin from 2003–2004. He is currently a doctoral candidate in sociology at the School of Education, Human Sciences and Law of the University of Derby, UK. He has a master's degree in education from the University of Leicester and also holds diplomas in social sciences and ELT, and a bachelor's degree in English language and literature from the University of Ankara. He has previously worked as lecturer, vice-rector and ministerial adviser in Turkmenistan, and in 2001 he received an award for cultural service to Turkmenistan. He is the President of the Institute of Interfaith Dialog, Houston.

Jill Irvine, formerly a faculty member of the Political Science Department, rejoined the University of Oklahoma in 2005. She teaches courses on Religion and Violence; Religion, Nationalism and Ethnic Conflict; Women and World Politics; Women, Religion and Secularism; and Feminist Theory. Dr. Irvine is the author of *The Croat Question: Partisan Politics and the Formation of the Yugoslav Socialist State* (1995) and co-editor of *State–Society Relations in Yugoslavia, 1945–1991* (1997). She has published articles in *East European Politics and Societies, Problems of Postcommunism* and *Politik* and contributed chapters to *The Extreme Right in Western* and *Eastern Europe* (1995), *Women in the Politics of Postcommunist Eastern Europe* (1999) and *The Dissolution of Yugoslavia* (2005). Her research interests focus on gender, democratization and ethno-religious conflicts worldwide.

Paul Weller is Professor of Inter-Religious Relations at the University of Derby and Visiting Fellow at the Oxford Centre for Christianity and Culture at Regent's Park College, University of Oxford. He is editor of *Religions in the UK: Directory 2001–3* (2001). Weller also contributed to a UK Government Home Office report entitled *Religious Discrimination in England and Wales, Home Office Research Study 220* (2001) and is the author of *Time for a Change: Reconfiguring Religion, State and Society* (2005), which drew on resources from the Baptist tradition of Christianity to argue against the establishment of the Church of England and for alternatives that are neither a defense of a "one-dimensional" Christendom nor the adoption of a secularist disestablishment.

Ali Bulaç graduated from the Istanbul Institute *of* Islamic Sciences in 1975 and from Istanbul University with a degree in sociology in 1980. He established Düşünce Journal and Publishing Company in 1976 and Insan Publishing Company in 1984. He co-founded the award-winning daily Turkish newspaper *Zaman* in 1986 and continues to contribute articles. He has published over thirty books including titles such as *Ortadoğu Gerçeği* (The Reality of the Middle East) (Istanbul, 1988), *Din–Felsefe Vahiy–Akıl İlişkisi* (Religion–Philosophy, Revelation–Intellect Relationships) (Istanbul, 2000), *Avrupa Birliği ve Türkiye* (The European Union and Turkey) (Istanbul, 2001), *Din, Devlet ve Demokrasi* (Religion, State and Democracy) (Istanbul, 2001), *Din ve Modernizm* (Religion and Modernism) (Istanbul, 2006).

Leonid Sykiainen Leonid R. Sykiainen graduated from Moscow State Institute of International Relations in 1969. In 1974, he received his Ph.D. from the Institute of State and Law, Russian Academy of Sciences. The subject of his dissertation was local government in Arab countries. In 1988, he took a higher scientific degree in legal theory with a dissertation on Islamic law. Between 1971 and 2003, he worked in the Institute of State and Law, Russian Academy of Sciences as a researcher, head of department and senior researcher. Since 2003 he has been Professor of the Department of Financial Law, Law Faculty, State University-Higher School of Economics, Moscow. He is also Professor of Moscow State Institute of International Relations, and since 2000 he has been a professor at the Institute of Asian and African Countries, Moscow State University. Dr. Sykiainen is the author of more than one hundred and sixty publications (books, articles, chapters, essays, conference papers) on Islamic law, comparative legal studies, theory and history of law and state, Islamic finance, human rights, and Islam in Russia and the Muslim world.

Ismail Albayrak graduated from the School of Divinity, Ankara, in 1991. With a scholarship from the Turkish Higher Education Council he completed his Ph.D. at Leeds University in the United Kingdom in 2000.

Since then he has been working as Associate Professor of Qur'anic Interpretation at Sakarya University, Adapazarı, Turkey. He teaches and writes on Qur'anic studies, classical exegesis, contemporary approaches to the Qur'an and orientalism. He is the author of *Klasik Modernizmde Kur'an'a Yaklaşımlar* (Approaches to the Qur'an in Classic Modernism) (Istanbul, 2004). His articles in English include "The Qur'anic Narratives of the Golden Calf Episode," *Journal of Qur'anic Studies,* 3 (2001); "The Classical Exegetes' Analysis of the Qur'anic Narrative," *Islamic Studies,* 42 (2003); "The Notions of Muhkam and Mutashabih in the Commentary of Elmalı'lı Muhammed Hamdi Yazır," *Journal of Qur'anic Studies,* 5 (2003); and "Turkish Exegeses of the Twentieth Century: Hak Dini Kur'an Dili," *Islamic Studies,* 43 (2004).

Joshua D. Hendrick received a master's degree in anthropology at Northern Arizona University and in sociology at the University of California, Santa Cruz, where he is now a doctoral candidate. His research focuses on the sociology and politics of religion, faith-based social movements, and issues of ethnic and religious nationalism. He is a research assistant on a research project funded by the Carnegie Foundation and entitled "Global Islam: State capacity and Islamist responses to globalization in seven countries." For the past four years he has researched the historical and contemporary development of Muslim politics in the Middle East and in Muslim-majority states. Currently, he is working on the impact and significance of the transnational movement of M. Fethullah Gülen.

Anna J. Stephenson is a graduate of the University of Houston with a master's degree in cultural anthropology. Her interests include using life histories to explore culture as experienced in everyday life as well as to encourage understanding between people of diverse backgrounds and viewpoints. Her research in the United States and Turkey focused on Muslim use of transnational spaces to influence the development of Muslim activism in Turkish society and national identity.

Bernadette Andrea is Associate Professor of English at the University of Texas at San Antonio, where she is also Chair of the Department of English, Classics, and Philosophy. Her research focuses on women's writing from the sixteenth through the eighteenth century, with a particular emphasis on Western European interactions with the Ottoman Empire. Her recent publications also focus on twentieth-century Algerian, Egyptian, and Turkish women writers. Her book Women and Islam in Early Modern English Literature is to be published by Cambridge University Press in 2007.

Mustafa Gökçek is a doctoral candidate at the University of Wisconsin–Madison. He received his undergraduate and then his master's degree in International Relations at Bilkent University, Turkey. His dissertation addressed Russian–Ottoman intellectual relations at the beginning of the twentieth century. His current research interests include the relationship between nationalism and Islamism, the development of Muslim communities in modern Turkey, and the Gülen community.

Introduction

Challenges in Understanding the Muslim Citizens of the Globalized World

Robert A. Hunt

The engagement of Muslims with the modern West has been the subject of increasing study by both Muslim and non-Muslim scholars. Muslim scholars have written for over a century about the appropriate response of Muslims to the West, and how Muslim engagement with modernity should shape an understanding of Islam. By the early 20th century Muslims understood themselves as part of intellectual, political, and social movements that sought either a restoration and renewal of the Islamic civilization of the 11th and 12th centuries, a return to the purity of the period of Muhammad and his immediate successors, or even a thoroughgoing "modernization" of Islam.[1] The names and self-understandings of these movements have changed through time and in relation to the rapidly changing circumstances of the

---

[1] Muslims themselves had several typologies to describe these various movements, and these have since multiplied with the addition of scholarly analysis from the West. Nineteenth and twentieth century Muslim reformers, such as Al-Afghani, Rashid Rida, Muhammad Abduh, Hassan al Bannah, Said Nursi and others consciously placed themselves within various traditions of Islamic reform and renewal beginning with the Prophet Muhammad himself. Later, writers such as Malik Bennabi, Said Nursi, Fazlur Rahman, Ismail Faruki, and Western scholars ranging from Bernard Lewis to John Esposito to John Voll and others would seek to further refine this analysis of reform movements. The result has been multiple typologies of such movements, as well as the recognition that reform and renewal have always been part of the Islamic tradition.

Muslim community. As this introduction is being written, scarcely a week goes by without a new analysis of developments in the Muslim world and a new approach to just which Muslim group is advancing which theory of how Islam should relate to modernity. Often these analyses are simplistic and politically motivated. Thus, "political Islam" is rather simplistically distinguished from "religious Islam" and "moderates" are distinguished from "fundamentalists," "radicals," or "terrorists." It is not uncommon for the whole Muslim world to be painted with a broad brush, with writers like Shelby Steele willing to say "the Islamic World long ago fell out of history," as if there had never been a serious engagement of Islam with modernity.[2] The threat of an Iranian nuclear weapon and the Israel–Hezbollah war in 2006 have turned attention to the differences between the Shi'a and Sunni in relation to reform and engagement with modernity, although that point has been made for decades.

While all simplistic analysis of the engagement of Islam with modernity should be rejected, some sympathy should be offered to both pundits and scholars. Four factors make it particularly difficult to analyze modern Muslim movements. The first is that the global reach of rapid communication has allowed charismatic Muslim leaders with new ideas about Islam to take those ideas from the margins to center stage with unprecedented speed. The media often add fuel to this fire, giving otherwise obscure leaders celebrity status and access to the whole world   with their ideas.

A second factor problematizing any analysis of the Muslim world is the realization that new ideas are emerging from Muslim societies long overlooked by both Muslim and non-Muslim scholars. Turkey, Central Asia, Southeast Asia, Europe, and Iran have often been treated as peripheral both to the Islamic world and the Muslim engagement with modernity—the historic importance of leaders from the sub-Continent like al-Afghani in the 19th century and Mawlana Mawdudi in the 20th century notwithstanding. Now terrorist links with Afghanistan, Pakistan, Indonesia, and Malaysia have brought Islam in these areas into the public consciousness, although the media seem to be scarcely aware of the full vitality of Islamic debate in those societies. Pakistan is seen as home to some "fundamentalist" movements to

---

[2] *Wall Street Journal* (week of August 24, 2006) Life and Death, by Shelby Steele.

be sure, but it is also home to other prominent voices from across the spectrum of Muslim self-understanding. Indonesia and Malaysia are both home to intense and varied debates on the meaning of Islam in the contemporary world. In these Muslim societies one is as likely to find a discussion of postmodern thought and the future of Islam as a discussion of purifying Islam from foreign influence. Turkey and Europe have emerged more slowly as recognized centers of Islamic engagement with modernity, perhaps because Turkey has long been a secular society by law and Islam in Europe is usually seen in terms of poor migrant workers. Yet, given the now longstanding interplay of Turkish Islam and Europe's growing Turkish minority, this should perhaps be reconsidered. And scholars both charting and seeking to guide the shape of contemporary Islam are emerging within both the European and the American contexts.[3] The case of Turkish Islam will come to the fore in the essays of this book.

The third factor which makes any analysis of contemporary Islam difficult is the rapid change in the environment with which Muslims are engaged. The works of Malik Bennabi and Fazlur Rahman could focus on Islam's engagement with modernity. Since they wrote, much of the West has moved (self-consciously, from an intellectual perspective) into post-modernity and new modes of self-understanding and religious and political engagement. Muslims engaged with the West, whether politically, economically, or intellectually, have been forced to adjust to these changes in the West.[4] Globalization in all its dimensions has led to a Muslim engagement with the non-Muslim world that is intense and multi-faceted. There are no mediators, except perhaps for the media, between most Muslims and the non-Muslim world. Widely varying cultural influences, technologies, political ideologies, and economic possibilities come directly to the doorstep of most Muslims with an implicit demand for an Islamic response. And Muslims themselves, as they have throughout history, are seeking out such engagement with the prospect of material, intellectual, and spiritual enrichment. The result is a world of ferment in which Muslims pioneer new

---

[3] Tariq Ramadan and Tarik Mitri in Europe, for example, and Muzzamil Siddiqi and Khaled el-Fadl in the United States.

[4] See the work of Ernst Gellner, *Postmodernism, Reason, and Religion* and Akbar S. Ahmed, *Islam, Globalization, and Postmodernity*, for example.

responses of varying degrees of adequacy not merely to the non-Muslim world, but to globalization itself.

The fourth and final factor making it difficult for many Westerners to fully understand contemporary Islam is the refusal of Muslim scholars and the movements they inspire to distinguish between the renewal of intellectual, political, and social movements in Muslim society. Thus, leaders like Mawdudi and Al-Afghani would both write on the renewal of the life of worship and belief, while founding enduring social institutions and political parties. In the highly integrated concept of an Islamic way of life held by most reformers, obligations to prayer, spiritual nurture, and social justice are of equal concern—as is the integrity of the life of the mind and the congruence of theology with the natural sciences. Rarely have Muslim reformers lived in ivory towers allowing their ideas to be parsed from their actions.

This collection of essays seeks to articulate some of the responses that have emerged from the Turkish milieu in the last half century. In one form or another the articles explore what has been called the Gülen movement, which is manifest in a growing body of intellectual discourse as well as a substantial social movement involving by some estimates over five hundred schools, a university, publishing and television outlets, and a growing network of institutions around the world devoted to interfaith dialogue. The movement takes its impetus from the works and teaching of Fethullah Gülen, a Turkish scholar and spiritual leader. Gülen's approach to Islam defies easy categorization, and part of his appeal is that he integrates the indigenous Sufism of Turkey, and in particular the teaching of Rumi, with a strong emphasis on orthodox Islamic belief and practice. In the tradition of Said Nursi, whose students make up a significant Muslim movement in Turkey and Europe, Gülen both recognized and sought to integrate with Islamic teaching the intellectual promise of modern science. Participants are not comfortable with militant laicist practices, but with him believe that Muslims can live fruitfully in and contribute to secular and religiously plural democracies.

While the Gülen movement is clearly significant within the Islamic world, and deserves more scholarly attention than it has yet received, it does face a number of challenges related directly to globalization. The articles in this book address some of these. In particular, it reflects the priorities of the

Gülen movement in addressing gender issues, the need for interfaith dialogue, the relation of Islam to secularism and democracy, and the application of Islamic principles in the realm of social and business life. Other important topics, outlined below, await more sustained attention by Gülen and those in his movement, and may be regarded as a future agenda for scholars seeking to understand fully the unique contribution of Turkish Islam to modern Muslim movements.

First, it remains for researchers to explore the Gülen movement experience of modern Islam as a multi-cultural, multi-linguistic phenomenon, and indeed as a civilization. There is a need for writing on the contemporary Islamic world comparable to Hodgson's work on Islamic civilization during the period from C.E. 800 to 1800, or the more recent work of Lapidus. With regard to the Gülen movement this will require several things, including (1) a further exploration of the role of non-Muslim religious minorities in dominantly Muslim societies, and (2) an exploration of the role of Muslim minorities in dominantly non-Muslim societies.

This will in turn entail a more serious study of the legacy of the Ottoman Empire, and how it was part of both the Islamic and European worlds. In particular, this exploration needs to be de-linked from the aspirations of contemporary Turkish national identity so that all aspects of Ottoman relationships with non-Turks and non-Muslims in its realms can be objectively explored.

It will also be necessary to place the Gülen movement in its social milieu and in particular in relation to Turkish social movements, both religious and otherwise. In particular, there is a need to understand better the relationship of the Gülen movement to the class of entrepreneurial businesspersons who provide financial backing for its institutions, have a strong interest in European integration, and play a distinctive role in the delicate interplay of society, state, and government in Turkey.

Finally, the movement will need to explore more fully Gülen's contribution to the dialogue of religion and science, taking more seriously the problem of a scientific worldview that completely denies the legitimacy of revelation as a way of comprehending the nature of the natural world and humanity. At this stage neither Gülen nor his followers have truly engaged scientists who are also philosophers of science. Scholars like Richard Dawkins, Steven Weinberg, Carl Sagan and others pose a serious challenge to

5

any religious approach to understanding. The legacies of Said Nursi and Fethullah Gülen will help Muslims meet this challenge but are not themselves sufficient. Closely related to this must be an exploration of Gülen's teaching to post-modernity.

In addition to these general challenges to placing the Gülen movement in context, there are particular needs with regard to the proven commitment of Gülen's followers to engage the multi-religious dimension of globalization through interfaith dialogue. The problem of interfaith dialogue in the contemporary world is largely the problem of competing meta-narratives. It is the problem of Western civilization claiming to provide the paradigm within which it can understand all other civilizations better than they understand themselves. It is the notion that science can understand religion better than religion understands itself. It is the notion that Christianity understands other religions better than they understand themselves, or that Islam understands Christianity and other religions better than they understand themselves. In the face of such meta-narrative claims, all dialogue essentially ceases because from within a meta-narrative there is no need to listen to the other. At the same time, globalization is rapidly making dialogue between holders of meta-narrative claims a near existential necessity. Western scholars have been working diligently on this problem for some decades. A distinctly Islamic contribution would be of great value in understanding how Muslims can fruitfully relate to globalization.

In a positive way, the essays in this volume remind us of how globalization can broaden scholarly horizons. In them one finds the intersection of three rather different worlds of scholarship, worlds which need to learn from each other before they judge each other. In addition to Western and Turkish scholars who have contributed to this volume, there is a contribution from Russia. The contribution from Russia reveals both presuppositions and experiences that are different from those of the West or the Muslim world. It seems to me that at the very least scholars need to take these perspectives seriously. Dialogue is always enriched when it brings together two very different approaches to understanding the same problem or issue.

This volume of essays brings into view a mix of Muslim and non-Muslim approaches to comprehending reality. For example, and at the root of all authoritatively Islamic thought, is the approach to understanding the

Qur'an and Hadith. Western scholars have not resisted the temptation to approach the study of the Qur'an and Hadith with so-called "literary-critical" methodologies. After all, this is the way that most contemporary Christian scholars approach the study of their scripture. Such an approach either doesn't acknowledge or it discounts the fact that Muslims developed an equally rational, one could say scientific, approach to interpreting the Qur'an and Hadith many centuries ago. Like literary critical approaches it is based on certain presuppositions about the nature of reality and how best to understand it. Christians have rarely sought to learn and appreciate this methodology, or that of the classical Islamic jurisprudence. They want to judge Muslim scripture from within their own post–Enlightenment framework. To fully grasp the contribution of Muslims to an understanding of the world it must be recognized that there is integrity between the scripture, the study of scripture, and the interpretation of scripture in each religious tradition.

There is a similar problem in discussions about democracy and society. The term democracy is often used as if it were a well-defined concept that transcends both differing worldviews and historical frameworks. In fact it is not. Contemporary American democracy has complex roots that are somewhat different from those of European democracies. It is marked by suspicion of all authority structures, almost total freedom of personal expression, confidence in a limitless capacity for human growth, a belief that some kind of religious commitment underlies all morality, and   a number of other characteristics that arise out of our complex relationship to a particularly Protestant-Puritan, particularly post–Enlightenment, particularly post–European, frontier experience. All the institutional aspects of democracy, such as elections, political parties, a balance of power in government, rule of law, and so forth, make sense only within the larger worldview of Americans. The same is true of democracy in Europe, which resembles American democracy, and yet is very different. Just one example: Americans talk about a "two party" system. Third party candidates are considered strange and somewhat threatening to democracy. But in Europe and most of the rest of the world countries often have dozens of political parties. The reasons for these differences come from vastly different historical experiences in the last two hundred years, but also from very different sets of religious ideas and ideals, and quite different worldviews.

This idea can be extended to something much closer to home for the Gülen movement. Numerous Muslim writers have found in central Muslim concepts of government—such as *shura*[5]—the basics of a democracy. And the constitution of Medina is seen by Muslims as a model of constitutional government. Clearly these are resources that will shape future Muslim understandings of democratic government. Yet, scholars must bear in mind that Muhammad and those whom he ruled in Medina lived within a historical experience and worldview so different from the modern West, or even the Muslim world, that it is hard to apply a single term like "democracy" to both. This does not mean, however, that talk about democracy between Muslims and non-Muslims is impossible. Rather, the whole of the lived human experience will need to be a resource for seeking out a shared human future. Recreating Athens, or Medina, or the Ottoman Empire, or the American founding fathers is not possible. But rediscovering and sharing the wisdom and insights that developed in those places is absolutely necessary if humans are to live and flourish together. And here there is a genuine resource in the study of Gülen and his place in modern Turkish political and religious discourse. The path toward democracy that Turkey has taken is substantially different from that of other nations, and it is shaped by a very distinctive cultural and religious heritage. Although Gülen is not a politician, he is shaping the consciousness that will determine the future of Turkish democracy. At the very least there is much to learn from that through interfaith   and intercultural dialogue.

This kind of dialogue that brings the whole of human experience to the service of the whole of humanity will require that people move beyond some well-worn ideas. Interfaith dialogue needs to embrace, but also to move beyond, the concept of tolerance. Islamic societies have generally tolerated non-Muslim minorities, but a society can tolerate others without actually engaging them or giving them a place as stakeholders in societal development. The same can be said of contemporary European and American societies. They are relatively tolerant, but remain disinterested in dialogue, learning from others, or in granting non-Westerners and non-Christians a significant voice in the unfolding transformation of civilization. The language and politics of tolerance is inadequate for Christian minorities

---

[5] Collective consultation.

in Muslim lands and Muslim minorities in Christian lands. And it seems that Gülen understands this when he invites non-Muslims to the table even though they are such a small minority in Turkey as to be politically insignificant. He gives them political significance in a way suggestive for the development of Turkish society, and Islam more generally

Gülen's approach to not merely tolerating, but empowering, religious minorities comes out of the Sufi tradition, which respected and learned from non-Muslim spirituality. The generous assumption that God is present in all religions and religious traditions is a basis for fertile dialogue. And here it must be mentioned that even as scholars turn their attention to Gülen's writings, it would behoove them to consider the writings of Christian, Jewish, Buddhist, and Hindu religious leaders who have been similarly generous in their appreciation of other religious traditions.

But to return to the Muslim Sufi tradition, it also offers a rich resource for overcoming the problem of competing meta-narratives. A hallmark of the Sufi tradition, and indeed almost all mystic traditions, is that they recognize transcendence beyond all religious conceptions of the Absolute. The Great Ocean of Being, the Absolute, the Real, all of these are understood in the Sufi tradition as provisional terms for Allah, Who is beyond the human capacity to understand or name. Gülen, like other great and generous saints and mystics, allows this humbling truth to guide him into interfaith dialogue. It allows him, and it can allow those inspired by him, to come to fellow humans not just as bearers of truth, but as seekers of truth.

There is a good deal of work yet to be done. This book and others like it have started to explore in a serious way, for the English-speaking world, the ideas of Gülen and the influence of the Gülen movement. The challenge for the future will be to explore how a genuine scholarly discourse can develop that is equally part of a lively interfaith dialogue. That will involve tackling some serious methodological issues that have not yet been addressed. The challenges mentioned above, and the ways in which they are addressed in the articles that follow, are only the beginning of placing this academic endeavor within a framework that is comprehensible both within and beyond the West. Still open to question is the larger problem of how scholars, coming from very different backgrounds and presuppositions, seek truth together.

As one of the co-editors of this work I find that this is of most interest to me. Rumi, the great inspiration of Gülen and his movement, wrote of the sighing of a reed flute that longed to return to the stream-bed from which it was plucked. I am not a mystic, and personally I do not feel a sense of loss and longing for the reed bed from which I was plucked. Were I a reed flute, I would be more interested in making music with a very human orchestra. This work, and those that undoubtedly will follow, are hoped to be the first efforts at making that kind of scholarly music.

The Regulated Potential of Kinetic Islam: Antitheses in Global Islamic Activism

Joshua D. Hendrick

Today we are in great need, above all else, of an objective mind which can see yesterday and today together, which can take humanity, life, and the universe into its perspective all at the same time, which can draw comparisons, which is receptive to the dimensions of the causes of and reasons for existence, which is cognizant of the scenarios of the rise, continuance, and fall of nations and communities, which can judge the errors, faults, and merits of sociology and psychology, which is alert to the rise, decline, and death in the cycles of civilizations.

M. Fethullah Gülen in The Statue of Our Souls

In this essay, I focus on the 20th century development of *Islamic activism*, the political and social mobilization of actors who deploy a specifically Islamic discourse to express their aspirations for social change. Islamic activism emerges when actors reform and renovate Islamic idioms to articulate modern political struggles and projects for social activism. Activists fuse the "structures of Islam" with the "structures of modernity" to express their social and political aspirations in non-alien terms. I outline the emergence of two ideologically and methodologically distinct forms of global Islamic activism, *global jihadist* and *civil/cosmopolitan*. I conclude with a brief analysis of the Turkish-based, globally expansive "service movement" of Fethullah Gülen. A civil/cosmopolitan mobilization, the Gülen Movement strives to present itself as exemplary in regard to the ways in which Islamic morality

11

and Islamic ethics might fuse with, rather than combat, the financial and political institutions of neo-liberal globalization.

Discourse Analysis, the "Other," and the Multiplicity of Modernity

According to Foucault, the purpose of discourse is to discipline populations, that is, to exercise power. The power exercised through discourse operates on a more sophisticated and clandestine plane than physical (i.e., coercive) expressions of power. Discourse defines the parameters of various and interlocked social structures, and subsequently informs the means by which individuals facilitate the reproduction of those social structures, the comprehensive and interconnected system of institutions and organizations that facilitate the continual reproduction of cultural, social, and political norms through the action and engagement of individuals. By defining and proselytizing social structures, the material effect of discourse presents itself in the regulation of human emotion and behavior. Once internalized, discourse has real material effects; when actors act under the auspices of a given discourse, discourse *becomes* reality. So how do the actions of individual Muslims collectively articulate to form some "thing" we may call "Islamic activism"?

Much of the scholarship on Islamic activism characterizes world history as a linear process of global modernization that begins in the West and moves to the rest. This view posits "Islam" as a unique culture and civilization that is structurally unable to integrate with the culture and civilization of the modern West (Huntington 1996; Lewis 1993; Pipes 2002). Islamic activism is viewed as designing and plotting a cultural and ideological counteroffensive to a century of perceived Western intrusion and domination. According to Samuel Huntington (1996:216–218), "the underlying problem for the West is not Islamic fundamentalism. It is Islam, a different civilization, whose people are convinced of the superiority of their culture and are obsessed with the inferiority of their power." The explanatory shortcoming of the "incompatibility thesis" stems from its proponents' refusal to analyze world populations as mutually constitutive within the context of a universally experienced temporal existence.

By contrast, Middle Eastern historian Reinhardt Schulze (2002:6) argues, "the major primary force of the Islamic world in the 20th century is

12

not Islamic culture (or even "Islam" itself), but the temporal context of modernism, which has deeply involved the political public in supranational world affairs." Schulze's notion of *universal time* suggests that although local events, local agents, and local processes can and do maintain local particularity, local events are, in part, expressions of larger processes occurring at the global level. No state, region, ideology, or belief system can be realistically designated as "pre-modern." Thus, modernism is "multi-lingual" and "the European dialect of modernism is merely one of many cultural dialects of modernism" (Shulze 2002:6–7).

In the 20th century, an unforeseen effect of European colonialism and subsequent state development in Muslim majority regions was the emergence of Islamic activist movements. In their effort to compete (politically, socially, and economically) in the modern world, Muslim intellectuals struggled to cultivate movements that could transform Muslim society by reframing traditional Islamic categories into a modern sociological existence. In this way, "Islam [became] a channel through which persons who had failed to become integrated into the secular system [of Ottoman modernization policies] were engaged in their own project of boundary expansion, and search for freedom" (Mardin 1989:83–4). Early theorists of Islamic activism needed to legitimate modern social and political organization using the sacred language of Islam, thereby creating socially and politically applicable Islamic idioms.

In order to understand the variation that exists across Islamic activist movements, it is first crucial to focus on the ways in which varying Islamic theorists seek to employ the signifying language of Islam so as to meet the structural demands of world systemic integration. This, coupled with the political and economic environments from which a particular activist movement emerges, determines the *regulated potential* from which *kinetic Islam* is possible.

Regulated Improvisation: Islamic Activism as Potential and Kinetic Islam

Habitus refers to the collection of structural possibilities, including cultural codes and signifying discourses, that provide the foundation for spontaneous individual and collective action. In the present era, habitus comprises the

13

structures of capital accumulation (production, class polarization, political liberalism, state (non)-regulation, etc.) and the structures of culture (religion, language, identity, etc.). Together these structures of habitus provide the means (i.e., discursive categories) by which humans mobilize for a collective purpose. The possibility for mobilization is limitless, in that varying expressions of specific structures are defined by an infinite number of regulated possibilities. The desire to innovate is constrained (*regulated*) by the structure (*habitus*) that comes before it. The desire to effect social change and to mobilize masses is regulated by the habitus of local, national, regional, and world history (Bourdieu 1977).

From the perspective of Bourdieu's notion of regulated improvisation coupled with Foucault's notion of self-replicating discourse, Islamic activism can be viewed as collective action that is defined by the habitus of Islamic modernity.

The organizational and spiritual dimensions of *Islam* (submission) first emerged in the 7th century on the Arabian Peninsula in the coastal oasis of the *Hijaz* (the stretch of land that includes Mecca and Medina). There, the first community of Muslims (*umma*) congregated around the Prophet Muhammad to form a new political community, and ultimately a new tradition in Abrahamic belief. Following the Prophet's death, and continuing throughout the history of Islam, "true Islam," in terms of legitimacy, practice, and identity, was widely contested in all sectors of Muslim society. For centuries, debates grappling with the transcendent versus universal nature of God's existence, the human capacity for free will, the veneration of Sufi saints, the legitimacy of Platonic rationalism, the development and subsequent adherence to legal systems, the political and religious role of the Caliph (Imam in Shi'a Islam), and so forth, were continuously contested, revived, and reformed. Immediately following the Prophet Muhammad's passing, Islam emerged in organizational, discursive, and spiritual multiplicity (Lapidus 2002).

Such multiplicity led Peter Mandaville (2001) to suggest that Islam should be viewed as a signifier that points to a wide variety of potential institutions, organizations, and practices, and in this way points to a "life-world" (i.e., habitus) that encompasses the social, political, and cultural histories of the Arab and Persian Gulf, Anatolia, North Africa, Andalusia, Central Asia, South East Asia, Europe, and North America, "[a life-world] whose borders are constantly changing" (Mandaville 2001:56). Drawing on Bobby Sayyid's (2004) notion of "Islam as master signifier," Mandaville contends that individuals throughout history have had access to a variety of categories and practices for them to draw upon when subjectively referring to themselves as "Muslims." Sayyid explains that his notion of Islam as "master signifier," is a discursive tool used by Islamic activists who seek to take advantage of Islam's potential to become a totalizing narrative:

> The ability of Islamists to articulate Islam as a central political category is not due, as some maintain, to the reputed indivisibility between politics and religion in Islam. Rather, it is the function of how Islamists attempt to transform Islam from a nodal point in a variety of discourses into a master signifier...the point to which all other discourses must refer. [Sayyid 2004:46–7]

Muslims (those who submit) refers to individuals who identify with a life-world that in part defines all Muslims the world over, and yet a life-world that provides the foundation for local and individual variation in regard to specific institutions, modes of practice, and personal expression of belief. In this way, Muslims exist in multiplicity, "in potential;" they are "Muslim" in so far as they subjectively internalize the discourse, history, and institutions of "Islam the signifier," and perform their improvised variation accordingly. Mandaville summarizes the interplay between "Islam the religion," "Islam the signifier," and "Islam the community of Muslims" as collectively comprising "the Islamic imagination," that is, the collection of competing narratives in Islamic history that struggle to claim legitimacy (if not dominance) over populations of self-identified Muslims:

> With the passing of the Prophet, Islamic political community ceased to exist and Muslim political community—as a space of negotiation—came to take its place. The very fact that today we find competing accounts of the Medinan period...bears testimony to its importance in the "Islamic imagination."
> [Mandaville 2001:73]

Expanding on Mandaville and Sayyid, I contend that diversity in Islamic institutions, Islamic epistemologies, and Islamic activism all collectively indicate that Islam exists discursively as *potential Islam*, and empirically as *kinetic Islam*. Kinetic Islam is the Islam that materializes (individually, organizationally, institutionally) in a specific social–political context, the regulated and improvised product of history. Potential Islam

15

refers to the diversity of past and present Muslim societies—to the habitus of millions of diverse individuals, organizations, and institutions, and to the scores of diverse spiritual and intellectual traditions—that is cited as source material for identity and social authority. A central observation in this study is that the processes and institutions of globalization (specifically, developments in information and communication technologies (ICT)) have exacerbated the potential for improvising upon the Islamic habitus to seemingly infinite kinetic proportions.

Categorizing Islamic Activism

What I am calling Islamic activism, others call "Islamism," while still others tend toward polemical categories such as "Islamic fundamentalism," "Islamic radicalism," "Islamic extremism," and so forth. The problem with these terms is that they do not allow for an examination of this phenomenon as it exists in its regulated multiplicity. While some actors, theorists, and organizations underscore hatred, violence, and intolerance and may very well be labeled "radical" or "extremist;" others underscore peace, tolerance, and dialogue. Neither "extremist" nor "radical" have the signifying capacity to connote such projects. Fundamentalism, as well, does not point to the social phenomenon as it exists in its complexity. Anthony Giddens (2000:67) defines *fundamentalism* as "beleaguered tradition…it is tradition defended in the traditional way—by reference to ritual truth—in a globalizing world that asks for reasons. In *Globalization and Its Discontents* (2002), Joseph Stiglitz complements Giddens' definition in his analysis of "market fundamentalism," (i.e., fiscal austerity, privatization, and market liberalization at the local and global level). Fundamentalism, according to Giddens and Stiglitiz, can apply to a variety of religious or secular beliefs provided they operate via blind faith to what is perceived as "beleaguered tradition."

Roy (1994; 2005) claims that, broadly speaking, fundamentalist *'ulama* (scholars) and the larger category of Islamic activists can be distinguished by their contrasting viewpoints on three primary issues: political revolution, *shari'a* (Islamic law), and women. In sum, Islamic activists believe in being socially and politically proactive while emphasizing the importance of participation in economic, political, and social spheres. Islamic activists subscribe to *ijtihad* (interpretation) in regard to shari'a and they reject the tradition of Islamic legal schools. In regard to women, Roy (1994:38) explains, "Islamists generally tend to favor the education of women and their participation in social and political life: the Islamist woman militates, studies, and has the right to work, but in a chador. Islamist groups include women's associations."

While my project incorporates a comparative historical analysis of the Gülen movement (GM) relative to political and social mobilizations organized explicitly under the rubric of Islamic categories, I do not suggest that the GM poses an *explicit* threat to existing political or economic institutions. However conservative, however devout, the GM is not fundamentalist. To avoid such an implication, I use *Islamic activism*, a term that includes all forms of socio-political mobilizations as they are defined through the habitus of Islamic modernity—be they antagonistic or not.

Project and Purpose: The Historical Development of Islamic Activism

Following the colonial retreat from the Middle East and North Africa, the urban middle- and upper-classes promoted and internalized a new sense of political identity and economic opportunity. Grounded in their nationalist agendas, governing regimes attempted to foster civic allegiance to the state by way of secular nationalism. What happened throughout the post-colonial Middle East and North Africa was a successful campaign by economic and governing elites to commandeer the ideology of social development. Because the European discourse on modernity, and subsequently the habitus of European modernity, managed to percolate through the middle- and upper-classes, most people in these societies "lost their power as world history makers" (Göle 2002:12).

World systemic integration brought with it rapid urbanization, whereby previously apolitical, rural, and predominantly poor collectives of Muslims found their way to urban centers. Secular state elites, unable to structurally compensate for the influx, failed to meet the employment, housing, and social welfare needs sought by the mass of urban migrants. In these new urban neighborhoods, European modernity was far from totalizing. Thus, not long after the close of the Second World War, secular nationalism ultimately proved to be a failed ideology in mobilizing the majority of Muslim populations:

> Between 1955 and 1970, population growth in the Muslim world
> approached 50 percent—a demographic change of spectacular
> proportions. By 1975, with urbanization and literacy advancing
> apace, the cohort under 24 years old represented 60 percent of the
> total population. The world of Islam, which had always been
> predominantly rural and governed by a small urban elite...now
> underwent a radical transformation. ...Social and political
> discontent was most commonly expressed in the cultural sphere,
> through a rejection of the nationalist ideologies of the ruling
> cliques in favor of Islamist ideology. [Kepel 2002:66]

While the Egyptian Muslim Brotherhood organized satellite organizations in Palestine and Jordan, most Islamic activist movements in the early 20th century were locally focused. It was not until the Soviet occupation of Afghanistan (1979–1989) that a truly global Islamic activist movement found expression. Around the same time, however, a small community of devout Turkish Muslims began to build schools across Anatolia, and eventually into Central Asia and the Balkans. The 1980s proved to be a pivotal time period in regard to the development of two seemingly competing forms of global Islamic activism—Al-Qaeda's global jihadism and Fethullah Gülen's civil/cosmopolitanism. While one refers to a multi-ethnic militant network of loosely connected insurrectionary groups, the other refers to a specifically Turkish, now globally active, network of educators, businessmen, journalists, and volunteers. Both refer to the regulated potential of kinetic Islam.

Global Jihadism versus Civil/Cosmopolitanism

In Islam, the community of believers is more than a religious concept; it connotes social solidarity and cultural identification beyond ethnic, regional, and state boundaries. In this way, the *umma* serves as the most fundamental of the concepts I have referred to above, concepts Şerif Mardin (1989) calls "Islamic idioms." Islamic idioms are shared paradigmatic concepts that serve the ultimate function of reproducing social structures over time and space (Mardin 1989:6–7). The Islamic idiom of the *umma* is significant to the extent that it underscores the theoretical universality of the Islamic habitus beyond family, tribe, and nation. All Islamic activism draws on the *umma* as the primary Islamic idiom to rationalize collective struggle for recognition in the modern era. As discussed above, however, despite their incorporation of similar language (i.e., despite their use of the Islamic discourse on modernity), the methods of engagement chosen by modern Islamic activist movements vary widely, depending on time and place (potential vs. kinetic).

On one end of the continuum, emphasis is placed on "greater jihad," that is, on the larger struggle with the self in regard to realizing the unity of God (*tawhid*) and the subsequent purpose of one's existence in unison with creation. Representative of this project in the early 20th century was the prolific Kurdish scholar and Islamic activist Said Nursi (d.1960). Nursi argued,

> Fanaticism, being violent and unreasoning devotion, is incompatible with Islam. However deep it is, a Muslim's devotion depends on knowledge and reasoning. For the deeper and firmer a Muslim's belief in and devotion to Islam…the further from fanaticism a Muslim is by virtue of Islam being the "middle way" based on peace, balance, justice, and moderation. [Nursi 1995:263]

Thus, Nursi viewed violence and intolerance as alien to Islamic epistemology, and thus incompatible with the project of Islamic modernity.

Such an understanding of jihad is contrasted significantly to the teleological and methodological perspective of global jihadists. Typified by Al-Qaeda and discursively organized by Osama bin Laden and Ayman al-Zawahiri, global jihadism legitimizes violent insurrection, not only against non-Muslim perceived oppressors, but also against other Muslims who are perceived as *kafir* (blasphemers). Such absolutism positions blasphemers outside the sphere of the *umma*, and subsequently discursively labels them non-Muslims. In the era of globalization, mass migration, and high-speed communication, the whole world is viewed as simultaneously entrenched in both the land of war (*dar al-harb*) and the land of Islam (*dar al-Islam*)— "apostates" and "true Muslims" are culturally and politically interwoven (Mamdani 2002).

Ontologically, global jihadists argue that liberal institutions, Western media, education, and lifestyle, and Western political leaders (and their puppet regimes throughout the Muslim world) are oppressive and dominating structures of social control. Together these structures are thought to be degrading the Islamist character of Muslim society and are collectively leading Muslims astray (by influence and by force) from not only their faith, but from their freedom. As indicated by the term "global," expressions of the

19

Islamist agenda in this form stress the significance of the global *umma* over and above any other possible subject positions. Nation and ethnicity are secondary to one's identity as Muslim. For global jihadists, oppression and persecution of Muslims in one locale are the same as oppression and persecution of Muslims everywhere. Although international pan-Islamic movements are observable throughout modern history,[1] global jihadism did not emerge in its mature form until the Soviet occupation of Afghanistan (1979–1989).

According to Mahmood Mamdani (2004:121), Afghanistan represents the "high point of the Cold War," in that American policy against Soviet occupation simultaneously exhausted the resources of Soviet power, and eventually brought to light "how the unintended consequences of misinformed, cynical, and opportunistic actions can boomerang on their perpetrators." Responding to an erroneous division of Islamist mobilization, between what Mamdani calls "revolutionary" and "elitist" Islamism, the CIA under the Reagan administration and in conjunction with Pakistani Central Intelligence (ISI) embarked on a mission to develop an internationally organized group of "Islamic guerillas" called the *mujahideen*. Funded in large part by the Saudi monarchy, the United States, and Pakistan, trained primarily by the CIA and ISI, and ideologically supported by figures such the Palestinian Sheikh Abdullah Azzam, the Afghan mujahideen included Muslim fighters from the Middle East, North Africa, Southeast Asia, Europe, and the United States who all assisted in the jihad against the Soviets.

Because of its reliance on the US for both strategy and infrastructure, Mamdani argues that what actually happened in Afghanistan was less a Muslim *jihad* for freedom than it was an American *jihad* for global dominance.

---

[1] *Pan-Islam* refers to the failed political project of 19th century Islamic modernism. Pan-Islamists attempted to seize Muslim identity and use it in conjunction with Islamic nationalism so as to instigate a globally unified movement of Muslim states against the oppressive onslaught of European colonialism. *Islamic Modernism*, in this sense, refers to the idea that modernity and Islam are not contradictory phenomena, but are mutually constructive. Nineteenth-century Islamic modernists argued that the Qur'an commands scientific inquiry so as to fulfill humanity's requirement to understand the glory of God, which is represented in his creation of Earth. According to Fazlur Rahman (1990:50–51) modernists argued "the West had cultivated scientific studies that it had borrowed largely from Muslims and hence had prospered, even colonizing the Muslim countries themselves. Muslims, in learning science afresh from the developed West, would be both recovering their past and re-fulfilling the neglected commandments of the Qur'an."

The United States tried to ignite Islamic populism around the world in a crusade against the Soviets, and "turn a doctrinal difference between two Islamic sects—the minority shi'a and the majority Sunni—into a political divide and thereby to contain the influence of the Iranian Revolution as a shi'a affair" (Mamdani 2004:128). What actually happened was that Muslims around the world were able to strive kinetically for an Islamic potential that had not been realized since the 7th century—*umma* solidarity. Beyond mere ideological solidarity, the Afghan *jihad* provided a means for military training, discipline, and the development of organizational and financial networks. The effective result of this experience, Mamdani (2004:130) explains, was that although claiming to "create an Islamic infrastructure of liberation…in reality [the US] forged an 'infrastructure of terror' that used Islamic symbols to tap into Islamic networks and communities." After the retreat of the Soviets, what emerged from this "infrastructure of terror" was Al-Qaeda (the Base); and, in the mid–1990s, Osama bin Laden emerged as its iconic leader.

What I call civil/cosmopolitan Islamic activism, others in the field call "liberal" or "moderate" Islam (Baker 1997, 2003; Kurzman 1998; Moussauli 1999; Sachedina 2001). By contrast to global jihadism, Charles Kurzman (2001:4) contends that there are numerous instances of individuals and mobilizations that, "oppose theocracy, support democracy, guarantee rights of women and non-Muslims in Islamic countries, [and] defend freedom of thought and the belief in the potential for human progress." I incorporate the term civil to connote the fact that these movements tend to focus their attention on civil society, rather than political insurrection. They tend to organize under the dictates of existing political structures, and they pose no explicit threat to contemporary political and economic systems. Cosmopolitan refers to the fact that these movements tend to advocate tolerance and dialogue with other social groups. As a contemporary development, re-articulation, and institutionalization of Said Nursi's discourse on Islamic modernity, the Gülen Movement is illustrative of the civil/cosmopolitan form.

The Rise of the Gülen Movement

On October 23, 1923, in Lausanne, Switzerland, the Allied victors of the First World War, led by Britain, signed a new treaty that formally recognized the demise of the Ottoman Empire, the creation of the Turkish Republic, and the legitimacy of the newly formed Turkish Grand National Assembly (Berkes 1998). The new republic based itself on the political philosophy of Mustafa Kemal "Atatürk"—the "six arrows of Kemalism"—populism, nationalism, republicanism, secularism, reformism, and etatism. Atatürk, appointed president for life, held the position until his death in 1938, and during his fifteen years in power, he and the Grand National Assembly implemented a series of top-down reforms so as to ensure the fruition of the Kemalist project. Some of the most notable of these reforms included the abolition of the Islamic Caliphate (1923), the outlawing of polygamy (1925), the outlawing of the Sufi orders and shrine veneration of Sufi saints (1925), the adoption of the Swiss civil code (1926), the outlawing of the fez and turban and the wearing of brimmed hats made mandatory for males so as to assure a secular nature to all male headgear (1927), the implementation of language reform, that is, Arabic script replaced with Latin (1927), female voting rights and the first female elected judges (1933–34) (Cleveland 2000).

One of the primary goals of Kemalism was to suppress the Ottoman–Islamic tradition from political and public culture. Kramer (2000:3) explains the profound nature of the Kemalist endeavor as "simultaneously an endeavor in state building…cultural revolution, and far-reaching social and economic change. Centuries of tradition became subordinate to a state-driven project of Western-oriented, democratically focused industrialization. In the new Kemalist state, realism became tantamount to culture, national identity emerged as primary over religious identity, and state-mandated liberal democracy marked the path for Turkey's development in the post–war world of capitalist states. Turkey's cultural and religious history was re-imagined in accordance with a new secular, modern, and republican "Turkish self." For this reason, political scientist Hakan Yavuz (2003a:7) argues, "contemporary Islamic movements in Turkey seek to re-claim the Muslim self.…Islamic movements produce, and are being produced by, new opportunity spaces for discussion where they can develop and experience novel lifestyles and identities." In the aftermath of the Republican period, and continuing after his death in 1960, one result of the Kemalist project was the rise of a community of followers who studied the teachings and texts of Said Nursi, the *Nurculuk* (followers of Nursi). In the early 1980s, liberal economic and political reforms created opportunities for a popular revival of Nursi's teachings and for the Nurculuk Movement.

The 1980 military coup was a watershed event in Turkish economic and political development. Responding to social violence on all sides of the political spectrum, the military arrested an estimated thirty thousand in the coup's first month alone. Internationally, Turkey found itself accused of political repression, arbitrary arrest, torture, and other human rights violations. The architect of the stabilization and transformation regime was Turgut Özal, a conservative bourgeois technocrat brought in to restore the governing autonomy of the Turkish elite. The expansion of the GM in the early 1980s was the result of two structural opportunity spaces opened under the Özal regime. First, Turkey's economic liberalization schemes gave rise to a conservative central Anatolian bourgeoisie. Second, the 1982 constitution opened up new spaces for social and religious organizing. Such social reforms opened doors for previously restricted religious expression, and led to religious revival throughout the country.[2]

Throughout the 1980s, members of the new Anatolian bourgeoisie, inspired by the teachings of Fethullah Gülen, began to invest in the construction of learning institutions across Anatolia. In the 1990s, political and economic development in Turkey provided the GM network with global routes to be explored. The fall of the Soviet Union, the structural weakening of the Turkish state monopoly over information and capital flows, increased Turkish migration to Europe, and global developments in ICT all contributed to the transformation of the GM from a modest community of Nursi followers to an international civil/cosmopolitan Islamic activist movement (Kuru 2005).

---

[2] The Özal regime emerged under the dictates of the 1982 constitution, which followed nearly three years of military rule in Turkey. The revival of Nursi's teachings, and other public expressions of religion, was a product of the constitution's amended bill of rights, which covered the social, economic, and political liberties of Turkish citizens. Among the more relevant were as follows: Article 5 stipulates all individuals are equal before the law and possess "inherent fundamental rights and freedoms which are inviolable and inalienable." Articles 28 and 67 stipulate that individuals have a right to privacy and to freedom of thought, and that the news media are free and not liable to censorship without a court order, which can only be obtained "when national security or the 'indivisible integrity of the state' are threatened." (Library of Congress)

The Gülen Movement in Thought and Practice

Fundamental to Islamic modernity is the tradition whereby Islamic activists reframe science and progress as Islamic idioms. Continuing the tradition of Said Nursi, Fethullah Gülen teaches that not only is modern science legitimate from the point of view of Islam, but advances in science prove nothing more than the reality of God's totality. Gülen (2004d: 142) argues, "religion, being a bountiful basin for science with its sources of knowledge, is an essential element, an important dynamic, a guide that has a clear method in matters that go beyond the horizons of knowledge." Science and Islam are viewed as two versions of the same story; one does not (cannot) falsify the other.

Incorporating the Turkish term *cehalet* (ignorance), Gülen argues that humanity has strayed from the righteous path of Islamic morality by forgetting the primacy of Qur'anic revelation and Prophetic example:

> Those who perceive religion as being contradictory to science and reason are the afflicted; they are unaware of the spirit of both religion and reason. Moreover, it is absolutely fraudulent to hold religion responsible for clashes between different sections of society. Conflicts between peoples and groups of people arise from ignorance, from ambition for personal advantage and profit, or from the vested interests of particular groups, parties, or classes. Religion neither approves nor condones such qualities and ambitions. [3]

Gülen contends that in the modern era humanity lacks *irşad* (moral guidance) (Agai 2003). Exemplified by the perfection of the Prophet Muhammad, moral guidance necessitates tolerance, dialogue, and understanding. Tolerance and dialogue are central to the GM's conception of reality and its identity:

> Among the many things we have lost, perhaps the first and most important is tolerance. From this world we understand embracing people regardless of difference of opinion, worldview, ideology, ethnicity, or belief. It also means putting up with matters we do not like by finding strength in a deep conscience, faith, and a generous heart, or by strength of our emotions. [Gülen 2004d:46]

---

[3] http://en.fgulen.com/content/view/1958/12/

The union of tolerance, moderation, and dialogue is collectively referred to as *hoşgörü* (literally "nice-seeing;" compassion). Adhering to *hoşgörü*, and actively promoting its qualities in both thought and practice, drives every aspect of the GM's international activities. For Gülen (2004d:98), "ideal humans...love and embrace everyone; they turn a blind-eye to the faults of others, while at the same time they are able to question the smallest faults of their own." In this way, *hizmet* (service) is central to the organization's vision of itself. Despite the apparent secularity of their activities, teachers, writers, and fundraisers all claim to be no more than "volunteers" who are actively engaged in hizmet to the ethical and moral transformation of the world.

The utopian project guiding the GM's collective action is to facilitate the emergence of a "golden generation" of "ideal humans" to serve as leaders in the era of the global village. Contradicting Samuel Huntington's assertion (1997:256) that "Muslims have problems living at peace with their neighbors," Gülen defines the movement's project as follows:

> In a world becoming more and more globalized, we are trying to get to know those who will be our future neighbors....One of the most important factors here is to eliminate factors that separate people...such as discrimination based on color, race, belief, and ethnicity....Education can uproot these evils. ...We are trying our best to do this. [Ünal and Williams 2000:329–331]

Although operating in an explicitly secular modern world system, and seemingly engaged in a variety of secular projects, the GM's mission is understood by its followers to be a spiritual quest:

> If we want to analyze religion, democracy, or any other system or philosophy accurately, we should focus on humanity and human life. From this perspective, religion in general, Islam in particular, cannot be compared on the same basis with democracy or any other political, social, or economic system. Religion focuses primarily on the immutable aspects of life and existence, whereas political, social, and economic systems or ideologies concern only certain social aspects of our worldly [i.e., secular] life. [Gülen 2004d:219]

Because "truth" is understood through Islam, "worldly life" poses no threat to the reality, identity, or purposes of the movement.

Methodologically, the GM strives to fulfill its sacred mission in a variety of ways. In 1994, followers of Gülen started the Journalists and

Writers Foundation, a non-profit organization that organizes national and international conferences on the attributes and benefits of interfaith dialogue (www.gyv.org.tr). Activists in the GM manage an expansive media network and are active in the construction of clinics, research institutes, and cultural foundations around the world.[4] Much of these institutions' success is due to the GM policy of working in accordance with its host country's national laws regarding education, religion, and social organizing, which can be seen as a deliberate articulation to adapt to diverse local contexts.

The primary methodological focus of the GM lies in the construction and operation of its nearly seven hundred schools worldwide. In the schools, GM teachers work to educate adolescents and teenagers in mathematics and in the natural and physical sciences. Özdalga (2003:103) elaborates on how the GM improvises the habitus of Islamic modernity at the level of the individual by explaining that for many GM teachers, education is subjectively understood as equivalent to prayer, "the teaching profession, thus conceptualized, is based on a combination of intellectual considerations (learning and teaching) and religious considerations (the ethics of giving)." In this way, Gülen educators seem to be acting out a form of "piety through work," similar to the Protestant ethic observed by Max Weber. Exemplifying the civil/cosmopolitan form, GM teachers act in accordance with Gülen's teachings, treating faith as a matter of personal religiousness. Civic engagement is viewed as an external expression of that religiousness in the form of dedication, diligence, hard work, and service:

> Who knows, maybe in the near future, thanks to these volunteers who devote themselves to letting others live…people will regret having fought each other over nothing, an atmosphere of peace

---

[4] Followers operate *Zaman*, the third largest newspaper in Turkey. *Zaman* was the first Turkish newspaper to become available on the Internet, and has won several major international awards for its journalistic integrity, newspaper layout, and design (http://www.zaman.com). The GM also operates a Turkish TV station, *Samanyolu TV*, and manages several major publishing houses, which together publish a variety of journals that emphasize a range of topics, from science and technology, to the environment, to an international English-language journal that focuses on Islam, peace, and interfaith dialogue (www.fountainmagazine.com). Rooting the financial structure is *Asya Bank*, an interest free "Islamic banking" institution opened in 1996 with less than US$1 million in startup capital, *Asya Bank* now has eighty-one branches in Turkey, and in May 2006, went public with 20% of the Bank's assets offered in its initial public offering (www.asyabank.com).

that was not previously established in the marketplaces…nobody's blood will be shed and the weak will not cry. [Gülen 2004d:214]

In stark contrast to the stated goals and methods of global jihadism, the GM illustrates an almost effortless ability to connect its improvisation on the habitus of Islamic modernity with the Euro-American dominated world system, thus highlighting the kinetic variation of potential Islam.

It is important to recognize that although the GM deploys a global discourse in regard to its Islamic project, it is a specifically Turkish movement. In addition to the movement's struggle to become ideal humans, its teachers and volunteers view Turkishness as a fundamental aspect of their identity. This is because the political and economic development of Turkey is organically connected to the GM's improvisational ability. Materially, the cohort of Anatolian capitalists that root the GM's financial enterprise, and who are the primary investors in GM schools around the world, are the heads of Turkish companies that have enjoyed significant growth since the early 1980s. In many ways, the growth of the Turkish economy equals, in part, the growth of the GM. Identifiably, GM schools around the world are known locally as "Turkish schools," and students at these schools are often enrolled in Turkish-language classes. Students also volunteer at international Turkish-focused events in their countries. Politically, the centrality of Turkey in regard to the movement's thought and practice, coupled with the Turkish government's recognition of the schools' success around the world, indicates that although the GM is not a specifically political organization, its activities nonetheless have significant policy implications in regard to Turkish relations in host countries, and Turkish investment in local and national economies.

The GM's Turkishness illustrates the fact that in Turkey, a society rooted in over two hundred and fifty years of structural modernization and secularization, the 20th century tradition of Islamic activism progressed along its own specifically Turkish path of regulated improvisation. Although suppressed by the early Kemalist regime and its processes of republican secularization, the folk traditions of Anatolian Sufism survived. Among the most significant of these survivals emerged in the form of Said Nursi and the Nurculuk. Over the course of the 20th century, continual processes of political and economic liberalization created the spaces for these survivals to adapt. The GM is illustrative of the fact that, "a majority of Turks do not perceive a contradiction between Islam and their attachment to Kemalist symbols, viewing both as integral to national identity" (Zubaida 1996:10). The sociological result of this dialectic is a Turkish–Islamic synthesis, a strong identity uniting Turkishness with Muslimness into one subject position, a merging of Turkish (European) and Islamic modernities (Yavuz 2003a). In this way, the GM emerged as the most successful purveyor of Turkey's improvisation of Islamic modernity, a civil/cosmopolitan Islamic activist movement that seeks to realize its goals of global transformation via "moral investment" in the global economy, "moral education" in the physical sciences, and moral convergence with "other" groups via tolerance, dialogue, and service. In a world consumed with religious and political extremism, the potential significance of such a movement's diffusion should be of interest to international policy analysts, social theorists, and religious scholars alike.

Conclusion: Globalization, Islamic Activism and the Gülen Movement

All forms of Islamic activism are indicative of the fact that the "imagined community" of the *umma* is experiencing a process of discursive materialization via a globally connected network of information, finance, and labor exchange occurring on the infrastructure of modern capitalism. While both drawing on and complicating Wallerstein's notion of "reactive ethno-nationalism,"[5] Lubeck explains how Islamic activists of all sorts socially construct multiple and identities within the context of "world systemic forces:"

> Over the long historical *duree*, the networks of the global *umma* are renewed annually by the pilgrimage to Mecca and, in the contemporary era, by the infrastructure of global capitalism. At the level of the territorial political unit, the emirate, sultanate, or the nation state, Muslims have an identity defined by the polity that administers Islamic law, *shari'a*. While the ideal is the abstract norms governing the universal *umma*…Muslims recognize that state-administered political institutions are necessary to enforce Islamic Law. [Lubeck 2000:154]

---

[5] According to Lubeck (2000), "reactive ethno-nationalism explains how subject peoples simultaneously invent new identities in order to contest the costs exacted by the accumulation processes of the capitalistic world economy.…Islamic identities, while subject to these processes, are more complex" (154).

Although locally bureaucratized and often locally focused, civil/cosmopolitan Islamic activist organizations illustrate the greatest degree of synthesis in regard to the fusion of what Bobby Sayyid calls the "master signifier" of Islam with the "master signifier" of European modernity.

In this paper I have attempted to illustrate the ways in which Islamic activism is an aspect of neo-liberal globalization, a modern development of activist movements that ranges across the Muslim majority world, a range that includes both global projects for confrontational revolution, and global projects for non-confrontational moral transformation.

Islamic activist networks such as that of the civil/cosmopolitan Gülen movement exemplify the postulates and assumptions of Manuel Castells' *Network Society* in the age of information and real-time globalization:

> What characterizes the current technological revolution is not the centrality of knowledge and information, but the application of such knowledge and information to knowledge generation and information processing/communication devices, in a cumulative feedback loop between innovation and the uses of innovation. [Castells 2000:31]

Fethullah Gülen and his movement of service-oriented volunteers seem to have successfully and innovatively manipulated the habitus of the information age with the habitus of Islam to develop what might be termed an "Islamic ethic of Capitalism." The movement provides evidence for both the varying capacity of Islamic activism, and the structural links that exist between what are so often perceived as fundamentally contradictory life worlds, that is, the West and Islam. Representing both Islam and Turkey, Muslims and economic liberals, nationalists and global citizens, the volunteers that make up the Hizmet network of Fethullah Gülen highlight the increasingly complex reality that Muslims and Muslim politics flow around the world with the same extensity and velocity as global capital, and are fundamental components of the 21st century global habitus.

The Educational Philosophy of Gülen in Thought and Practice

Yüksel A. Aslandoğan and Muhammed Çetin

Today everyone and every organization is working for some specific goal. I serve people in a way appropriate to myself within the framework of my belief....Human beings are the most honorable of creatures. Those who want to increase their honor should serve this honorable creature.

Fethullah Gülen in Advocate of Dialogue

The land where the world renowned poet and Sufi Master Rumi lived and taught is now witnessing an unprecedented development with global effects. Teachers, parents, and business owners are participating in a socio-cultural movement which is primarily driven by activism in the field of education. This civic initiative has been inspired by a Turkish Muslim scholar, M. Fethullah Gülen, whose humble beginnings gave little indication of his potential. Over the years, Gülen has encouraged the social elite and community leaders, industrialists, as well as small businessmen, to support quality education. With donations from these sources, educational trusts have been able to establish hundreds of schools, both in Turkey and abroad.

The educational philosophy of Gülen is the source of inspiration of the movement. It can be said to have four dimensions. The first is a paradigm shift: a new appreciation for the enterprise of education and the profession of teaching, elevating both to a noble status. Gülen presents education as the only lasting solution for society's problems and the needs of humanity. Teachers who embody the universal values cherished by parents are the primary agents of civic activism. The second is altruism, or the elimination of selfishness and establishment of community service spirit in the field of

31

education. The third is the social dimension, which brings together the educator, the parent, and the sponsor in a tripartite relationship for the altruistic service of humanity through education. Finally, in the epistemological dimension we see a synthesis of the heart and the mind, tradition and modernity, and the spiritual and the intellectual. We see an approach to education that is at peace with science and technology, as it warmly embraces the culture and beliefs of society at large.

As will become apparent through our discussion below, these dimensions are closely connected with each other. The ideas, beliefs, premises, or actions in one make the others work reciprocally. While the world has no shortage of educational models or theories, a distinguishing feature of the educational philosophy of Gülen is the fact that it has not remained in speeches or books only.

It should be noted that the schools inspired by Gülen's educational understanding are not religious or Islamic. Instead, they are secular private schools inspected by state authorities and sponsored by parents and entrepreneurs. They follow secular, scientific, state-prescribed curricula and internationally recognized programs.

For the lack of a better or more concise name, these schools are sometimes called "Gülen schools," a term Gülen personally finds inaccurate and inappropriate, and never condones. He says, "I am tired of saying that I do not have any schools" (Webb 2000:106).

While the roots of this educational movement lie in Anatolia, or modern Turkey, the world-wide popularity of the schools points to the fact that Gülen's educational paradigm has universal appeal. High achievement in math and sciences and emphasis on the exemplary moral character of teachers and its impact on the children's behavior are among qualities often praised by parents.

The Role of Education

Gülen sees education as the primary solution to the three problems that plague developing countries, namely ignorance, poverty and division (Ünal and Williams 2000:319–320). Gülen asserts that knowledge, work-capital, and unity can combat these. As ignorance is the most serious problem, it is defeated through education, which has always been the most important way of serving one's own community, country and humanity. Poverty is eliminated through work and the possession of capital. Internal schism and separatism are eradicated through unity, dialogue, and tolerance (Çetin 2005:16). Gülen emphasizes:

> As the solution of every problem in this life ultimately depends on human beings, education is the most effective vehicle, regardless of whether we have a paralyzed social and political system or we have one that operates like clockwork. [Gülen 2004d:202–209]

In Gülen's vision, education is the institution that can help eliminate ignorance and endow people with knowledge of their environment as well as a sense of purpose in life that will guide them in their relationships with their environment. Education is the vehicle by which a higher sense of identity can be developed to end divisions and frictions over insignificant differences.

> Gülen believes the road to justice for all is dependent on the provision of an adequate and appropriate universal education. Only then will there be sufficient understanding and tolerance to secure respect for the rights of others. [Woodhall and Çetin 2005:viii]

Finally, education, when properly designed and implemented, has the potential to turn citizens into productive and industrious participants in the economy. We will discuss below Gülen's vision of an educational enterprise that can deal with each of these problems by involving every segment of the society. Çetin (2005:5) maintains that "rather than dealing with daily politics, Gülen makes the latent and dormant power in the Turkish people visible and forces it to assume a shape in terms of educational, health, and intercultural and interfaith services and institutions."

A Holistic Approach to Education

One way to evaluate Gülen's educational philosophy and its appeal for diverse societies from Turkey to South Africa, and from the Philippines to Romania, is to review what first motivated his philosophy and activism. Gülen was born in the eastern city of Erzurum during the early period of the newly formed Turkish Republic. He studied at a public elementary school until the third grade. Due to his father's appointment to a village where there was no public elementary school, he could not attend the remaining grades in

33

elementary school and obtained a diploma later through passing comprehensive examinations. While Gülen mostly continued his secular education through self-study, he always remained a keen observer of the public education system (Ünal and Williams 2000:322).

Gülen sees education as "a humane service." He says, "We were sent here to learn and be perfected through education" (Ünal and Williams 2000:319). He holds education to be the only lasting solution to the problems facing his society and humanity at large. But in order for education to fulfill its mission, four aspects of the educational enterprise needed to be addressed: the first was the lack of a synthesis of the heart and mind, faith and reason, or science and religion.

> At the root of the predicament of the modern society lies the separation of the heart and the mind in education and scientific thinking. [Gülen in Ergene 2006:309]

In Gülen's view, the formal education system in Turkey has never been promising (Ünal and Williams 2000:323), and contemporary schools have failed society in failing to infuse their students with ethical and spiritual values. As a consequence of this failure, those in charge of scientific and technological development pursued selfish ends instead of serving the needs and interests of society and humanity (Gülen 2000:77).

Second, there was a need for high scientific, professional and moral standards of teachers, accompanied by an exemplary personal, professional and idealist paradigm of life and work (Gülen in Ünal and Williams 2000:310).

> Gülen therefore helps nurture a movement dedicated to education, but an education of the heart and soul as well as of the mind, aimed at reviving and invigorating the whole being to achieve competence and providing goods and services useful to others. [Woodhall and Çetin, 2005:xi-xii]

The third was the lack of public support and participation in education. The solution to the problems plaguing society was an overall improvement in education, in Gülen's estimation. He insisted that this could not be achieved in the hands of a political elite who were estranged from society. Instead, altruistic teachers who view education as a noble profession and the formation of an educator–parent–sponsor triangle were essential. Teachers, administrators, educational policy-makers, parents, sponsors such as entrepreneurs, and civic leaders, in short, almost every segment of society, needed to play a role in this grand social project (Ünal and Williams 2000:325).

Finally, Gülen lamented the politicization of education, science and technology. Webb discusses the period in Turkish history during which Gülen grew up and crystallized his understanding of education and services as follows:

> The problems of education and health have been Turkey's two most important issues since the period of the Ottoman State. The problems continually grew larger during the republican period and were even manipulated for political goals. What aggravated the situation was that ideological and political concerns rather than logic and science ruled almost all the decisions made in the field of education. During this time, Turkey never became a noteworthy country in this field in the international arena. To the contrary, the universities, which should have done high-level scientific work, each became a point of political focus and were in the forefront of the three military coups d'etat. [Webb 2000:1]

The Purpose of Learning

Throughout his public life, Gülen has insisted that learning is an obligation on all humans:

The main duty and purpose of human life is to seek understanding. The effort of doing so, known as education, is a perfecting process through which we earn, in the spiritual, intellectual, and physical dimensions of our beings, the rank appointed for us as the perfect pattern of creation. [Ünal and Williams 200:305]

According to Gülen, the purpose of learning lies in satisfying human and community needs and solving the problems of the world:

> Given the great importance of learning and teaching, we must determine what is to be learned and taught, and when and how to do so. Although knowledge is a value in itself, the purpose of learning is to make knowledge a guide in life and illuminate the road to human betterment. Thus, any knowledge not appropriated for the self is a burden to the learner, and a science that does not direct one toward sublime goals is a deception. [Gülen 2004d:17]

35

Through his motivational efforts Gülen focused the attention of his audience on education, and put education on the national agenda. Gülen's proactive approach to the development of education and the kind of altruistic activism that he championed promised to make education a potent tool for solving the problems of society. He said:

> I encouraged people to serve the country in particular and humanity in general, through education. I called them to help the state educate and raise people by opening schools. [Gülen 2000b:320]

Altruism as a Motivating Force in Education

Gülen's motivational efforts started initially with teachers and potential sponsors. He went to great lengths to motivate college students to choose education as their profession. He saw altruism as the key to convincing business owners and entrepreneurs of the feasibility of sponsoring educational projects.

> Today, a transcending responsibility that falls on our shoulders is to rekindle the altruistic desire to let others live in the hearts of our fellow citizens…In such an activism, there is a need to identify a set of shared values that will form the trajectory of such a broad social action which will include all segments of the society, the villager and the city dweller, the intellectual as well as the merchant, the student as well as the teacher, the lay person as well as the preacher. [Gülen in Ergene 2006:330][1]

Gülen motivated his audience by reminding them that each of them was already a teacher. His broader concept of teacher included not only classroom teachers in public schools but many other key personalities, from prophets to parents, from the philosopher to the dervish, from the lover of wisdom to the government administrator (Ergene 2006:312). According to Gülen behind every great person in history was a great teacher.

Gülen's message to teachers and prospective teachers was simple: serving your fellow citizens and humanity in general through education is a duty for every responsible human being and fulfills the purpose of our creation. Suddenly, the relatively low-paid, unappreciated, and low social

---

[1] Translated by Aslandoğan.

status teachers were being recognized as the key builders of the country's future. Gülen's motivational addresses to teachers highlight his vision for the role of education in a better future as well. He encourages volunteers to,

> devote themselves to letting others live, [so] the mind and soul will embrace each other once again, conscience and logic will become complementary depths of each other, physics and metaphysics will stop fighting and withdraw to their own realms, and everything will find the opportunity to express the beauty in its own nature through its own language, the intricacy of legislative rules and the principles of creation will be rediscovered. [Gülen 2004d:214]

For the faithful in his audience, Gülen drew motivating examples from the Muslim prophetic tradition. He often mentioned the prophetic saying that the only valuable knowledge in God's sight was the knowledge that benefited humanity (Ünal and Williams 2000:331). He referred to another prophetic saying that curing a person who has a terminal disease may be more valuable than one thousand sessions of optional prayer; he was alluding to the opinion that it was a duty upon every Muslim to alleviate the suffering of fellow human beings regardless of their religion, nationality, or location on the earth. The examples he drew on from Islamic history and other Islamic sources offered abundant examples of how service to humanity was valued by God (Gülen 2004d:4). This perspective empowered Gülen's audience to commit unprecedented energy and enthusiasm to the service of society through educational projects without religious instruction, indoctrination, or discrimination.

Representation over Presentation

An important principle of Gülen's educational philosophy was representation. According to Gülen, only teachers who embodied universal values could achieve a successful synthesis of the heart and the mind.

> Real teachers...occupy themselves with what is good and wholesome and lead and guide the children in life and whatever events they encounter. ...In addition to setting a good personal example, teachers should be patient enough to obtain the desired result. They should know their students very well, and address their intellects and their hearts, spirits and feelings. [Gülen 2004d:208]

Barton (2005:28–29) describes how this representation covers all aspects of life. The Gülen movement applies this practice in mass media, ethical banking and education. In this way, their practice embraces all aspects of life and different individuals through such services

Gülen's Synthesis of Tradition and Modernity, and Religion and Science

A primary feature of Gülen's educational philosophy was his successful formulation of a middle way in the presence of radical approaches to a multitude of social issues. He witnessed a rationalism devoid of spirituality that focused exclusively on self-interest. The other extreme was a blind adherence to tradition. His middle way in this context was underlining the necessity of sound reasoning for every individual while promoting spiritual values as a guide for the intellect. Between self-centered individualism and collectivism he defined a middle way that inculcated a sense of social responsibility that did not neglect or deny individual rights. He promoted serving one's community as a responsibility of being human and conduct pleasing to the Creator. At the same time, he framed individual rights as uninfringeable for the greater good without an individual's consent. (Kuru 2003:115–130)

But perhaps the most crucial synthesis Gülen was able to achieve in theory and in practice was his proposal for a harmony of science and religion, reason and faith. The view of science and religion as categorically contradictory or antagonistic to each other, to him, is a shallow one: those who perceive religion and science in this way are unaware of the spirit of both religion and reason (Gülen 2005a:20).

> In recent centuries, the religion–science conflict has occupied many intellectual circles. Enlightenment movements beginning in the eighteenth century saw human beings as mind only. Following that, positivist and materialist movements saw them as material or corporeal entities only. As a result, spiritual crises have followed one after another. It is no exaggeration to say that these crises and the absence of spiritual satisfaction were the major factors behind the conflict of interests that enveloped the last two centuries and reached its apex in the two world wars. [Gülen in Ünal and Williams 2000:314]

In Gülen's discourse, science and faith are not only compatible but complementary. Gülen saw the faith-based worldview as providing a comprehensive and sound narrative[2] that could support and give meaning to learning.

> The best sort of knowledge to be acquired in the school must be such that enables pupils to connect happenings in the outer world to their inner experiences. [Gülen 1998:99–100]

Religion encourages knowledge for understanding oneself and the universe while providing a general framework and a source of inspiration and direction "to order individual and collective life, so that we can attain real happiness here and in the Hereafter" (Gülen 2000b:91). While it would be futile to expect religious texts to detail scientific inventions, it would be equally ignorant to reject the possibility that the text might hint at new inventions, technologies, and insights (Gülen 2000b:99).

> Only the love of truth, defined as approaching existence not for material advantage or worldly gain but to observe and recognize it as it really is, gives true direction to scientific studies. Those with such love will achieve their goal; those who do not have such love, who are led by worldly passion, material aspiration, ideological prejudice, and fanaticism, either will fail or turn science into a deadly weapon to be used against whatever is best for humanity. [Gülen 2000:77]

Gülen also rejected the view of religion as blind faith. The Qur'an certainly did not ask of its readers to accept matters of faith without the use of reason and intellectual scrutiny.[3] On the contrary, it criticized those who failed to use their reason and to explore and analyze the observable universe. While acknowledging the important role of reason, Gülen also pointed out its limitations: logical reasoning needed premises and information. Incorrect premises or information would inevitably lead to the wrong conclusions. Besides, the reasoning mechanism itself was prone to errors called logical

---

[2] For a detailed discussion of the term *narrative* and its role in motivation, see Neil Postman, *The End of Education: Redefining the Value of School,* Vintage, New York,1995.

[3] For examples, consider the following verses of the Qur'an: Signs in nature for those who reflect, 2:164; 3:190–191; 10:5–6; 12:105; 13:3–4; 16:10–16, 66–69, 78–81; 17:12; 29:44; 30:21–24; 39:42; 45:3–5, 13; 51:20–21; Humans urged to use reason and understanding, 2:73, 242; 3:190–191; 6:151; 30:24; 45:5; 67:10; Humans urged to reflect and ponder, 3:191; 7:176, 184; 10:24; 16:44; 30:8; 34:46; 59:21; 4:82; 23:68; 38:29; 47:24; Criticism of failure to use reason, 2:44; 5:58; 8:22; 25:44; 36:62.

fallacies. Considering these limitations, it would be ignorant to reject religious assertions as contrary to science and reason without considering possibilities for reconciliation. Hence, from Gülen's point of view, the supposed antagonism between reason and faith was in reality a conflict between blind faith and deficient reason.

The second type of perceived conflict was of a factual nature. Some assertions in religious sources were perceived as contrary to scientific findings and vice versa. Gülen (in Ünal 1998) dealt with this type of perceived conflict by analyzing and examining examples of such conflicts and showing that each case could be explained by a gap in the scientific explanation or a misinterpretation of the religious source. More systematically, he argued that perceived factual conflicts between science and religious sources would inevitably be found to be due to one of the following causes:

1. A gap in the scientific explanation, such as uncertain data or an over-generalization, or mixing of personal opinions with hard scientific facts.

2. Unauthentic or weak religious sources, or a gap in our understanding of religious sources, such as a misinterpretation, lack of a holistic understanding or mixing of personal opinion with authentic revelation.

3. The pursuit of a non-scientific agenda under the disguise of science.

4. The pursuit of a non-religious agenda under the disguise of religion.

Motivating Parents and Sponsors

Gülen's successful synthesis of tradition with modernity and his persuasion of teachers to work in education with full commitment, self-sacrifice and in an altruistic manner helped attract parents and sponsors towards the educational institutions inspired by his thinking. This attraction produced a virtuous cycle: successes of the schools in science competitions (biology, math, physics, chemistry, computer, theory or projects) provide positive publicity, which in turn attracts more parents, sponsors, and support from local authorities.

> The business circles of the movement are the main sponsors of these schools, supporting them financially until they are able to

raise their own revenues through school fees. In each country, the community works in co-operation with the local authorities, who often provide logistical assistance and supervise the curriculum. [Woodhall 2005:3]

While Gülen's understanding aimed to contribute to public education in general through a new generation of teachers, it was recognized that this would take time. As part of this process, he encouraged business owners and entrepreneurs initially to sponsor dormitories where students could stay and study together under the tutorial and supervision of qualified and educationally dedicated teachers. Secondly, he promoted the widespread sponsorship of college-preparatory courses in the regions as well as in the major cities in Turkey, a country where quality college education provided a primary means of upward economic and professional mobility. Finally, he promoted private school projects which were secular and which would work within the state's framework of unified education. Parents send their children to these secular but private schools despite the load tuition places on budgets already strained under harsh economic conditions. For secularly oriented parents, it was simply a question of cost–benefit analysis: "Is it worth the extra money to send my child to such a private school?" The success of the schools in national and international competitions and the ratio of graduates getting into reputable colleges, as well as the fact that the students are not susceptible to negative aspects of youth culture such as drug and alcohol abuse, removed any doubt in the minds of parents.

For the faithful, on the other hand, there was another question: "Why should I send my child to a school with a secular curriculum instead of a state-run Religious Studies school?" The answer was convincing: in accordance with the requirements of the state educational policy, the schools would not teach religion. Instead, teachers would embody the universal values the parents themselves cherished, such as truthfulness, trustworthiness, respect for parents and the elderly, respect for one's heritage, and love of every human (Ünal and Williams 2000:348).

Gülen's argument was the equivalent of one familiar to western readers: "Actions speak louder than words." If children witnessed integrity, hard work, truthfulness, trustworthiness, caring for others, generosity, respect for law and human rights, and abstinence from bad habits and all intoxicating substances, they would not need explicit instruction in these universal virtues. Teachers who exemplified the importance of being law-abiding and moral accountability for one's actions and one's treatment of fellow human beings were more effective than text books and instruction. As for the details of worship and rituals, Gülen suggested that the parents were responsible for living and teaching them either during early childhood or at home.

The accomplishments of the Gülen-inspired schools and college-preparatory learning centers had another impact. These successes led to the formation of a nationwide atmosphere of competition that was unheard of during the period when public schools were the only choice people had. Suddenly, rich entrepreneurs saw private schools as viable business ventures and began to establish their own private schools apart from the Gülen movement. Other faith-oriented and secular groups joined with their own initiatives following the example of Gülen-inspired schools. In this sense, Çetin (2005:37) maintains that the Gülen movement is a progenitor movement in that it sets original models and successful examples which other movements copy and emulate (Zald 1996:269).

Gülen's Own Altruism

Another factor in Gülen's successful motivation of teachers as well as parents and sponsors was his own ascetic life and altruism. Gülen was a distinguished scholar coming from a very modest background. With no ambition for worldly wealth, and as a person of God, a preacher, a man of spirituality, asceticism and profound knowledge, he could have had a very satisfying career simply serving as a community leader and author. However, he concentrated his effort on motivating the masses to invest in sound education and has led by example. He has never had personal wealth to be able to sponsor educational projects. Instead, he has appeared at fund-raising dinners and visited wealthy individuals to convince them of the importance of sound and modern education. "I have no power, capital, or army—only an unstoppable love and enthusiasm for service. All I can do is explain this, tell those who will listen, and suggest" (Ünal and Williams 2000:326).

In the past, Gülen had served as a teacher, supervised students and personally cared for the social, mental, intellectual, and physical well being of students in dormitories under his supervision. Now, despite health problems such as diabetes, hypertension, and cardiovascular disease, he continues to inspire and guide individuals working for educational projects through the media and his writings, editorials and interviews, and private meetings.

In addition to never having any personal wealth, he is reported to have prayed for his relatives to remain poor so as not to raise any suspicions of gaining from his influence. His relatives reputedly laugh and say that "as long as *Hocaefendi* is alive, we have no hope of becoming wealthy!" (Gündem 2005).

Woodhall observes that every school has its own independent accountants and accountancy system. They are all answerable to the local authorities and the trust's inspectors, and comply with the state and international law (Woodhall 2005:4). Apart from encouraging people to donate money, Gülen has carefully remained distanced from their financial management and instead encouraged their sponsors actively to oversee the use of their contributions. This has built enormous trust and confidence in Gülen's honesty and integrity and also in the people employed at the Gülen-inspired institutions.

Avoidance of Politicization

The participants in the Gülen movement, and the schools they have established, avoid involvement in partisan politics, and this is reflected in their educational projects. Gülen has always maintained his non-partisan stance, although political leaders often consult him. He is against the instrumentalist use of religion in politics, and he has strongly encouraged people around him to remain out of direct involvement in politics. He has remarked:

> We are equally distant from each political party and equally close to each of their members. [Ünal and Williams 2000:277–278]

Gülen's philosophy was very simple, when the country is already suffering from various forms of division, education should remain an island of unity. The virtues and successes of the educational projects should not be tainted by association with political ambitions or party political activism (Barton 2005:2; Ünal and Williams 2000:320).

Since the beginning of the Republic, the attitude of the Turkish intellectual elite has been that education is too important an enterprise to be left to the masses (Howard 2001:103–107). They could never imagine that large numbers of business owners and entrepreneurs might sponsor private education without asking for anything in return. Indeed, some individuals, though very marginal, still question the funding of the schools and look for foreign sponsorship or illegitimate means behind it, whether because of ideological polarized views, or for fear of losing the politically and economically vested interests they have been long enjoying, or out of straightforward malice and grudge against Islam and any initiative coming from Muslims or faith-based communities, or out of lack of foresight.[4] This same attitude was responsible for producing an educational and technocratic elite that was alienated from large segments of Turkish society (Ataman 2002:122; Secor and O'Loughlin 2004:11; Yavuz and Esposito 2003:xiv). Gülen's approach, on the other hand, tapped into the patriotism, productivity, and industriousness of a nation that had proved its civic contribution in the Turkish War of Independence (1919–1922) and in the establishment of the Turkish Republic. Despite dire conditions then, and despite the fact that the country had been engaged in wars for the past two decades, the Turkish nation fought and gained its freedom from occupying French, British, Italian, Russian/Armenian, and Greek forces. Gülen's persuasive approach combined with his own altruism, his avoidance of partisan politics, and his total lack of interest in taking credit "makes the latent and dormant power in the Turkish people visible and forces it to assume a shape in terms of educational, health, and intercultural and interfaith services and institutions" (Çetin 2005:5).

Establishment of the Educator–Parent–Sponsor Relationship

One of the crowning achievements of Gülen in his activism was the establishment of the tripartite educator–parent–sponsor relationship (or family–school–environment, Ünal and Williams 2000:310). But this achievement was only possible because of two other main factors.

First, to be involved in education, the society was looking for an educational philosophy that embraced their cultural heritage and values, instead of trying to eliminate or replace them. Gülen's thinking was anchored in tradition but embraced modernity without fear. As Turkish society was in a quest for an education that endowed their children with modern knowledge

---

[4] For more, see Çetin 2005.

and skills while preserving their values, Gülen-inspired schools offered an education excelling in math, science, language, arts and sports while retaining the common moral values. Gülen maintains:

> A community's survival depends on idealism and good morals, as well as on reaching the necessary level in scientific and techno-logical progress. [In addition], trades and crafts should be taught beginning at least in the elementary level. A good school is not a building where only theoretical information is given, but an institu-tion or a laboratory where students are prepared for life. [in Ünal and Williams 200:310]

Secondly, the public wanted to make sure that their financial contributions were not wasted. Gülen's emphasis on the altruistic approach of the educators and the embracing of this attitude by a generation of young teachers gave the public this much-needed confidence.

As his approach entailed serving the whole community, Gülen persuaded parents who were paying tuition and the business owners supporting the schools that the educational opportunities offered to the financially-able families needed to be extended to the economically disadvantaged. As a result of the establishment of scholarships, between twenty and forty percent of the enrollment in these schools consisted of children whose families could not otherwise afford to send their children to private schools. The sponsors understood that they were paying for the education of not only their own children but additional economically disadvantaged students as well, and they embraced this approach cheerfully. Some parents and financial sponsors even took the extra step of establishing scholarships for tens or hundreds of additional students. Gülen's premise was that philanthropy was not alien to the human soul, but that the soul needed to be convinced that its contributions would not be wasted.

Publications and Media for the Education of Society at Large

Recognizing the fact that the schools addressed the educational, social, and affective needs of only a part of society, Gülen also encouraged the establishment of publications and media institutions that would serve the whole society in a manner similar to the public radio and TV stations in the United States of America.

> People who want to guarantee their future cannot be indifferent
> how their children are being educated. The family, school,
> environment, and mass media should cooperate to ensure the
> desired result. Opposing tendencies among these vital institutions
> will subject young people to contradictory influences that will
> distract them and dissipate their energy.
> [Ünal and Williams 2000:310]

While not receiving any funds from the government, these
publishing houses and media institutions would have the education of the
society as their utmost goal instead of profit-making. Hence, Gülen
encouraged people from many walks of life to get together to establish
various forms of mass media institutions to contribute to the construction of
public discourse through interactions.

Examples of such publications and media institutions include a popular
magazine on the synthesis of religion and science (*Sızıntı*), another on environmental
issues (*Ekoloji*), one on literature (*Yağmur*), one on religious sciences (*Yeni Ümit*), a
children's magazine (*Gonca*), a high-quality newspaper with ten world language
editions (*Zaman*), a radio station (Burç FM), a TV station (STV) and a leading
publishing house (Kaynak A.Ş.).[5]

Gülen encourages and inspires the use of mass media to inform
people about matters of individual and collective concern and to aspire to
greater visibility in the decision making processes which govern the media
and define the social agenda (Çetin 2005:16–17). When talking about the
qualities of the new type of people who would embrace all humanity with
altruistic services, Gülen says:

> To stay in touch and communicate with people's minds, hearts,
> and feelings, these new men and women will use the mass media
> and try to establish a new power balance of justice, love, respect,
> and equality among people. They will make might subservient to
> right, and never discriminate on grounds of color or race. [Gülen
> 2004d:82]

The unifying traits among these publications and media institutions
were the elements of their publication policies. Examples of these elements
include zero tolerance for sensational or graphic violence, obscenity, or
glorification of bad habits or intoxicating substances, but balanced spaces for

---

[5] For more on the media initiatives, see Çetin 2005:15–18.

46

education, information, art, culture and entertainment, separation of commentary from reporting, and pursuit of accuracy in information as opposed to misreporting, to concern with ratings, or to manipulation of reality (Pope 2005:372; Bonner 2004:96–97; Murphy 2005).

What Makes Gülen-inspired Schools Attractive

Among the motivating factors for teachers, parents and sponsors of the educational projects, we identify three attractive features of Gülen-inspired schools:

1. A satisfactory combination of tradition and modernity including science, reason, and technology, and proven academic achievement in these fields.

2. The altruistic approach of the well-qualified and well-trained teachers and educators, and the lack of profit-seeking.

3. Non-politicization of educational, scientific, and cultural issues, institutions and efforts.

Woodhall lists three factors in explaining the appeal of the Gülen-inspired schools both in Turkey and increasingly around the globe:

The schools in Turkey and elsewhere invariably follow the national curriculum, even in countries where private schools may be exempt from such a requirement. In addition to being unusually well equipped for the teaching of science they tend to have very good English language departments and small classes. These three factors are seen as key to the ultimate educational and professional success of the pupils and are vital factors in the marketing of the schools to the growing educated middle class in Turkey, Central Asia, and other non-English speaking countries. [Woodhall 2005:4]

As for the management of affairs, all these institutions are independent corporate bodies. There is no formal relationship among educational institutions or the other institutions, both within and without the country, except where there is a chain run by an educational trust. The institutions disperse news of their accomplishments through the mass media and promotions. In this way, ideas and thoughts that arise from a commitment to the same feelings are shared and owned by all (Tekalan 2005:6).

International Successes for Increasing Self-Efficacy

The educators who are working in the Gülen-inspired institutions are encouraged to see each student as a separate world. They consider one-to-one interaction with individual students to be the basic tool of education, and they allocate most of their time to their students (Tekalan 2005:5).

In addition to setting a good personal example, teachers should be patient enough to obtain the desired result. They should know their students very well, and address their intellects and their hearts, spirits, and feelings. The best way to educate people is to show a special concern for every individual, not forgetting that each individual is a different "world." [Gülen in Ünal and Williams 2000:312–313]

By participating and succeeding in international competitions such as science Olympiads, the psychology of despair and the lack of self-confidence in developing countries or regions is replaced with self-efficacy.[6] Expert teachers are hired when necessary to help prepare students. The fact that world Olympiad champions in math and sciences have been educated by these schools all over the world is evidence of this self-efficacy (*Zaman* 2006). A case in point is Salih Adem, a former student of a Gülen-inspired school in Izmir, Turkey, who won the gold medal in the International Physics Olympiad (IPHO) twice (1993 USA and 1995 Australia) and was the winner of the youngest participant prize in IPHO history (1992 IPHO).[7]

Woodhall (2005:5) points out a secondary positive aspect of such competitions—that the pupils' success in mathematics and science is important in publicity and marketing of the schools. She concludes, "it is only the remarkable harmony between Gülen's philosophy of education and the cultural practice of his followers which can explain adequately the continuing growth and success of the movement" (Woodhall 2005:23).

---

[6] Bandura defined *self-efficacy* as "individuals' confidence in their ability to control their thoughts, feelings, and actions, and therefore influence an outcome" (Bandura 1994:71–81).
[7] Turgut 1998.

Supportive Environment, Mentors, and Peer Culture

The Gülen-inspired schools do not succeed in math and sciences at the expense of language, arts, or sports. Instead, they provide an environment supportive of a fulfilling educational experience. An important consideration in these schools is the attention to student welfare and accommodations. The environment is designed in a holistic manner to minimize the time students spend in fruitless activities that do not help with their education. Material structures such as high quality dining rooms, dormitories, libraries, multi-media rooms, and sports facilities combine with the availability of qualified tutors and mentors to make the schools ideal places for supporting learning.

Following the example set by their educators, some ex-students come back to their institutions on their own initiative to tutor and help current students. Tekalan observes:

These educational institutions have helped young people to complete their undergraduate and postgraduate studies and to participate in active integration in the society where they live. …As the young people who were educated at these institutions started to work at the same institutions as their teachers and administrators, the process accelerated. [Tekalan 2005:3–4]

The peer tutoring activities are one of the schools' strategies for creating an environment where peer culture values academic success and where parent involvement is high. As in the analytical studies conducted by Steinberg since 1985, parent involvement, peer culture, and opportunities for concentration are key elements in student engagement (Steinberg 1996; 1997). In addition to his writings about the importance of teachers' characters and the early environment of the child, Gülen has recognized the influence of the student's peer group:

Having faithful friends is just as important as satisfying the vital necessities of life. Being among a secure and peaceful circle of friends means finding safety against many hazards and dangers. [Gülen 2000a:66]

Teacher Development

Among the factors that lead to high achievement in Gülen-inspired schools, we can mention teacher in-service training programs. In these programs academics, expert teachers and tutor colleagues train teachers in course presentation techniques, teaching methodology, educational and classroom management, student needs and psychology, and curriculum design. Both teacher-training and student preparation programs are supported at times by hired expertise, such as experts in science Olympiads, university professors, and personal development professionals (Woodhall 2005:5–7).

The self-training of teachers is also supported through sponsoring participation in national and international educational conferences and seminars. The publications of the various educational institutions invite teachers to take part in the development of instructional materials. This participation in turn enables teachers to remain up-to-date in their expertise fields.

Finally, the institutions employ equal opportunity employment practices. This means that the movement is open to employing individuals who are skilled at their jobs but who would not identify themselves as Gülen movement participants. This allows the movement to maintain a permeable boundary with the outside world.

Prevention of Substance Abuse

The General Director of the Kyrgyz Turkish schools, Yücel Bozkurt reports:

> People become addicted to alcohol and cigarettes at a very young age. We try to turn our students away from this road by holding conferences on the health hazards of such addictions. We make cooperative efforts with their parents, and have obtained very good results.[8]

Interviews conducted with parents from various countries where Gülen-inspired schools operate point to the significance given by these parents to the policy of zero tolerance on intoxicating or addictive substances on school campuses (Ünal and Williams 2000:349). For instance, in an interview, Mr. M.D., an administrator at a Gülen movement school in a capital city in Eastern Europe, related the following experience:

> The school board had recently decided to expel a certain student due to his continued misbehavior disrupting education and setting a bad example. His father, however, was determined to keep him

---

[8] http://en.fgulen.com/content/view/780/13/

in the school. In the following days, we received phone calls as well as visits from various officials, such as members of the parliament, the mayor, and high-ranking government officials. The school board finally decided to give this student a second chance. He would still be expelled from this campus. But he would be allowed to register at another campus of the same school system in another city. The father accepted this decision cheerfully. Out of curiosity, I asked the father why he went to such great lengths to keep his son in our school. His answer was simple: "My son has a weakness for drugs. I do not believe that I can keep him away from drugs in any other school but yours."

Education Against Terrorism and Intolerance

On terrorists, Gülen has commented that:

> There must have been something wrong with their education. That is, the system must have some deficiencies, some weak points that need to be examined. These weak points need to be removed. In short, the raising of human beings was not given priority. In the meantime, some generations have been lost, destroyed, and wasted. [Gülen 2004a:6–7]

One of the strategies to overcome conflicts and tensions which may lead to terrorism is social inclusiveness. Gülen writes:

> Be so tolerant that your bosom becomes wide like the ocean. Become inspired with faith and love of human beings. Let there be no troubled souls to whom you do not offer a hand and about whom you remain unconcerned. [Gülen 1998a:19]

The enactment of this in the schools is exemplified in the following incident narrated by the sociologist Nevval Sevindi about the experiences of an administrator of a Gülen-inspired school in southeastern Turkey. It serves as an example of the positive role of tolerant and inclusive educators:

> Speaking Kurdish, [the general director of the school] established a close relationship with [two new students] and listened to their problems. He gave them something to eat and drink and a place to sleep. However, for fifteen days these two boys became very unruly. They broke windows and destroyed furniture. Later on, it came out that their purpose was to make the principal angry and after being beaten or thrown out, they would say: "Turks treat us like this." However, being treated in such a loving way finally

51

caused them to admit: "They told us so many negative things that we hated you. We came to burn the school but we couldn't." [Ünal and Williams 2000:332]

Sevindi also tells of a letter which she received while she was working for the Turkish daily *Yeni Yüzyil:*

> One student from Cizre (a town in southeastern Turkey) wrote in a letter: "I always saw Turks as our enemy until the Preparatory Course opened. I liked all of you a lot. If you had come here before, maybe there wouldn't have been any terror. My uncle went to the mountains; maybe he wouldn't have gone." [in Ünal and Williams 2000:332–333]

In countries with religious, cultural and ethnic diversity, the Gülen-inspired schools function in part as bridge builders. They establish the foundations of dialogue and mutual understanding among individuals and communities (Ergene 2006:313). Thomas Michel, the secretary for Inter-Religious Dialogue of the Society of Jesus in Rome, gives the following account of a Gülen-inspired school in the Philippines:

> My first encounter with one of these schools dates back to 1995, in Zamboanga, on the southern Philippine island of Mindanao, when I learned that there was a "Turkish" school several miles outside the city. On approaching the school, the first thing that caught my attention was the large sign at the entrance to the property bearing the name: "The Philippine–Turkish School of Tolerance." This is a startling affirmation in Zamboanga, a city almost equally fifty percent Christian and fifty percent Muslim, located in a region where for over twenty years various Moro separatist movements have been locked in an armed struggle against the military forces of the government of the Philippines. I was well-received by the Turkish director and staff of the school, where over a thousand students study and live in dormitories. As I learned from the Turkish staff and their Filipino colleagues, both Muslim and Christian, the affirmation of their school as an institution dedicated towards formation in tolerance was no empty boast. In a region where kidnapping is a frequent occurrence, along with guerrilla warfare, summary raids, arrests, disappearances, and killings by military and para-military forces, the school is offering Muslim and Christian Filipino children, along with an educational standard of high quality, a more positive way of living and relating to each other. [Michel 2003:70]

Conclusion

Notable characteristics of Gülen's educational framework include a high status for the enterprise of education and the profession of teaching, an altruistic approach to service in education, the idea of reward-free sponsorship, non-politicization, successful combination of the scientific outlook with sound morality, and an emphasis on a healthy educational environment conducive to success in every field of human endeavor including science, math, arts, language, and sports. None of the activities of the Gülen movement schools breach the limits of the system or break the laws of the countries in which they operate.

These characteristics help motivate various stake-holders to form the tripartite educator–parent–sponsor relationship that propels the schools to success. Additional factors of attraction are peer-tutoring, educationally conducive accommodations, increased teacher availability, supportive peer culture, and participation in national as well as international competitions. A systematic approach to teacher development includes expert and peer-tutoring, teacher participation in instructional material development and the quick dissemination of best practice by professionalized networks and the media.

The Gülen-inspired schools prove themselves successful in the sight of communities in Turkey and abroad by mobilizing inactive, dormant, but innovative energies present in Turkish and other societies; by absorbing conflicting pressures and easing tension within fragmented communities; by subduing to common sense the potential for coercive means and ends that induce changes in political systems; by involving diverse people within a very short time over a large, extended geography, to achieve joint educational projects; by always progressing and modernizing its academic culture and educational organization; by raising or selecting new elites for the services provided; by employing a sound rationality through the visible neutrality of technical expertise in order to be able to appeal to all; by socializing and transmitting universal values; by having a large number of educational organizations operating across economic, political, and cultural borders; by peacefully transforming collective action and services into institutionalization; and, last but not least, by being a progenitor movement.

With their origins in Turkey but now widely spread and acknowledged around the globe, the schools established by Gülen-inspired participants increasingly function as bridge builders that help establish harmonious relationships among the members of their own society as well as the civilizations of the world.

We believe that Gülen, like Rumi, will be remembered as a great contributor to humanity. Much has been written and said about the overseas Turkish schools in both Turkey and in other countries.[9] It is certain that considerable time will be needed merely to understand and document what has already taken place within a period of almost thirty years.

Gülen deserves the last word:

> Education is the most effective and common tongue for relations with others. We are trying our best to do this; we have no other intention. [in Ünal and Williams 2000:331]

---

[9] In 2005, Ufuk Publishing, aiming to create an objective evaluation of Turkish schools, put the question "What do you think about the Turkish schools abroad?" to 27 intellectuals of different views, including former Prime Minister Bülent Ecevit, Professor Kemal Karpat, ret. Ambassador Gündüz Aktan, former Higher Education Board (YÖK) Chairman Professor Mehmet Sağlam, Professor M. Ali Kılıçbay, Kyrgyz Author Cengiz Aytmatov, Professor Ümit Meriç, Professor Mümtazer Türköne, film producer Halit Refiğ, journalist Gülay Göktürk, and Professor Niyazi Öktem. These intellectuals, almost all of whom had visited the schools and had the opportunity to speak directly with the students studying there, wrote down their views and assessments. The resulting book, *Bridges for Peace: Turkish Schools Opening to the World*, explains the thought and mass support behind the educational institutions opened in almost eighty-four countries in the world.

The Gülen Movement and Turkish Integration in Germany

Jill Irvine

This essay treats the role of the Gülen-inspired centers and schools in promoting a positive model for the integration of the Turkish community in Germany while allowing its members to maintain their cultural and religious roots. A great deal has been written in the past decade on the challenges of integrating the large Turkish community into German society. More recently, this has become part of a wider discussion about growing religious fundamentalism and violence among Europe's Muslim population. While this discussion has correctly highlighted the social, economic, and political barriers to integration presented by the host societies, very little has been published in English about the efforts among Europe's Muslim populations to promote their own visions and models for integration. Certainly, foremost among these models is the Gülen movement, which has embraced a modern, multicultural notion of political identity and community that is also deeply rooted in Muslim practice and traditions. To what extent have Gülen-inspired centers in Germany been successful in promoting this model of mutual co-existence between ethnic Germans and Turks?

The debate over Turkish-Muslim integration in Germany has revolved around three main educational policy issues. The first involves the role of religious instruction in the schools and how instruction in Islam can best be delivered to Muslim students. Religious instruction is part of the core curriculum in German schools and, while there is increasing recognition of the need to offer Islamic religious instruction, such instruction has also been highly contested. The second educational policy debate involves the

55

establishment of private Muslim or Turkish schools. Turkish students have typically performed less well academically and have been far less likely to attend a German college-preparatory high school; the establishment of private schools is intended in part to address this problem. Germans have a strong tradition of public school education, however, and the state and federal governments have resisted the establishment of private Muslim schools. The third educational policy issue involves the wearing of headscarves in the schools. While, in contrast to France, German schools permit female students to wear headscarves in the classroom, instructors in almost all areas of Germany are prohibited from doing so. This has become the subject of various court cases and continues, as does the role of women overall in Islam, to be a flashpoint for tensions between the ethnic German and Turkish-Muslim communities in Germany.

These policy issues raise the larger question of Turkish-Muslim integration and what it entails. As one scholar of European Islam put it "Until now there is hardly any 'German' or 'European' way of Muslim life generally accepted by Muslims and non-Muslims on a theoretical and social level which would keep the values and ways of Muslim belief as well as it would fit into the framework of society as a whole" (Rohe 2004:102). On the one hand, many German policy makers such as former Cabinet Minister and Parliamentary President Rita Süssmuth insist that their approach to integration distinguishes them from their counterparts in countries like France who emphasize the necessity of assimilation (Dowling 2006). On the other hand, many ethnic Germans and residents of Turkish descent alike charge that the German approach is one of assimilation (Stowasser 2004:61). To them, the vision promoted by such leaders as Bavarian Christian Social Union (CSU) leader Edward Stoiber is one that requires the minority Turkish population to do all the adjusting (Interview 1).

The numerous Gülen-inspired centers established during the past decade in Germany have attempted to find a "middle way" between the cultural devastation implied by assimilation and the "ghettoization" of a minority group living apart from the majority culture. For the teachers and staff of these learning centers, cultural centers, and schools, any solution to the challenge of integration must involve the give and take of cultural understanding and mutual enrichment. These residents must become educated according to German standards and fully capable of operating at the highest levels of German professional society, but the key to integration is to provide the best possible education, which is also "mindful" of Turkish culture. In the words of the Director of the Atlantic Learning Center, "The best method of integration? That's simple. Education!" (Interview 7).

This paper is based on research conducted in Germany in July and August 2006. During this period I visited several learning centers in Munich, Berlin, and Ingolstadt, a high school in Berlin, and an intercultural center in Munich.

I interviewed the directors of these learning centers and the school, as well as other staff and participants in their activities. My goal was to place the activities of these groups and centers in the larger context of the debate about integration of the Turkish Muslim minority in Germany. What vision of integration are they attempting to promote and how?

Description of Gülen Movement Activities in Germany

Gülen movement participants in Germany have founded a variety of educational institutions that operate throughout the country. There are three major types of institutions: learning centers, which offer after-school tutoring to students from elementary school through high school; intercultural centers, which sponsor a variety of programs and events to promote cultural and religious exchanges between residents of Turkish background and the majority German population; and more recently, private high schools, which offer a full college-preparatory curriculum to students primarily of Turkish background. The movement is not directly affiliated with, nor does it currently sponsor, any mosques in Germany.

Learning centers currently operate in most of the major cities and towns in Germany. While there is no Germany-wide source of statistics on these centers, the Director of the Learning Center in Ingolstadt guessed that there may be over a hundred centers in Bavaria (Interview 7). These centers typically serve about a hundred and fifty students at a variety of levels from grades 1–13, offering courses in German, English, math, and science. In addition, the learning centers offer a variety of adult courses. Parents of children receiving after-school help at the centers attend meetings at least once a month in which they discuss with teachers ways in which they can offer a supportive learning environment in the home. Several learning centers have also recently begun to offer "Integration Courses." These federally-mandated courses, now required of all immigrant adults, offer 600 hours of German language instruction and 30 hours of instruction in German culture and history over a six-month period. Turkish language instruction for Germans is also offered at the centers.

The staff at learning centers is drawn largely from university students of Turkish background. While the teachers are paid for their services, a significant component of their participation in the centers constitutes volunteer labor, since they do not receive the same pay that they would in a comparable tutoring position elsewhere. This is because the non-profit learning centers are entirely self-supporting through fees for courses and services. Unemployed parents may receive funding for their children to attend the center; however the centers generally do not, at the moment, receive direct financial support from the state and local governments.

Intercultural centers have been established in some of the bigger cities in Germany. They are specifically intended to sponsor activities that promote cultural and religious understanding and dialogue between the Turkish and German communities. While the stated goal is mutual interaction, the main point seems to be to expose Germans more to Turkish culture and society. Events and activities consist of lectures, trips to Turkey, Turkish language courses, participation in Round Tables and panel discussions, dinners for Germans hosted in Turkish homes and other activities for youths and adults. The centers are self-supporting through membership fees. The Intercultural Dialogue Center in Munich, established in 2001, has an active membership of 100. The intercultural centers (and other Gülen-inspired institutions in Germany) do not maintain close relations with other Turkish or Islamic groups. Mindful of their "inability to control the behavior and activities of these groups," and the extremist inclinations of some of them, the intercultural centers prefer to concentrate their dialogue and outreach activities on the Germany community (Interview 1).

The establishment of private schools has been a goal of Gülen-inspired activities worldwide, but until recently it was not possible to do so in Germany. The establishment of three private, college-preparatory high schools in Berlin, Dortmund, and Stuttgart in the past two years, and the anticipated establishment of three more high schools in the next two years represents a new phase of Gülen movement educational activities in Germany. These schools offer the same curriculum as public college-preparatory high schools with the difference that they offer Turkish as the third language choice, after German and English. (Depending on the high school, in Germany the third language is typically Latin or French.)

Learning centers, intercultural centers and high schools are typically governed by an association, which is regulated according to German law. The members of the association, typically parents of children involved or members of the Intercultural Center, choose a board of directors, generally consisting of seven members. Members of the board of directors, which have a two-year term, are represented by a president who must approve all major decisions concerning hiring of teachers and educational curriculum and policy. The board generally meets once or twice a month.

The relationship between the Gülen movement and the institutions described above is loose and one more of inspiration than organization. As in Turkey, the movement is extremely decentralized. For example, there appears to be no central record-keeping office for the Gülen-related institutions in Germany; each city or town is responsible for organizing and maintaining its own schools and centers. Moreover, many of the participants in the centers and schools appear to have no idea that they are inspired in any way by the ideas of Gülen. According to the head of the Wedding Educational Center, 80 percent of the parents are unaware that the centers are connected in any way with the Gülen movement since the staff does not typically talk about it with them. Indeed, he emphasized that most teachers are there because they believe in what the centers are doing, not because they are necessarily inspired by Gülen (Interview 3). The Director of the Learning Center in Ingolstadt estimated that more than fifty percent of the members of the Association but only two or three of the teachers have anything to do with the movement (Interview 7). In any case, every director and representative with whom I spoke was clearly influenced by the ideas and practice of the movement.

Religious Instruction in Schools

One of the most important issues concerning the integration of the Turkish-Muslim population involves the question of religious instruction. German Basic Law of 1949 provides for religious instruction in public schools and also for its regulation at the state level. The law stipulates that "religious instruction shall form part of the regular curriculum…in state schools" (Article 7, German Basic Law, cited in Fetzer and Soper, 2005:111). The curriculum, teachers, and materials for these classes are determined by the religious communities involved, primarily the Protestant and Roman Catholic communities. Parents usually choose whether to have their children attend classes in one of these two variants of the Christian faith (or where enough parents request it, the Jewish faith) or in a more general ethics class; in some areas parents may withdraw their children from religious or ethical instruction altogether.

In the past decade, there have been increasing calls from Muslim parents to allow their children to enroll in Islamic education classes. German authorities have become increasingly receptive to the idea as a way of fostering integration and avoiding less desirable alternatives. As one expert on this subject put it:

> It should not be forgotten that there is a certain concern among Muslims and non-Muslims about the existing alternative of private Qur'anic schools, which are partly run by persons or groups of an obvious extremist or anti-western observance. For this a system of reliable co-operation between the Muslim communities and the state, which puts Islam into the middle of "normal" school education, appears to be the only desirable alternative for the future. [Rohe 2004:97]

While Islamic instruction has been offered in some areas of Germany, several obstacles have impeded its introduction in most of the country. First, no Muslim group has yet achieved public corporation status, a special legal status extended to the Christian and Jewish communities under German Basic Law. The status affords the religious community certain rights and protections such as the right to have the government collect money from members of religious communities in order to provide financial support to those communities (Fetzer and Soper 2005:107). The lack of legal status for the Muslim community has meant that school authorities do not feel obligated to provide religious instruction to their Muslim students. Second, school authorities point out that they do not have a clear partner to work with in devising a curriculum and appointing teachers. The Muslim community in Germany, while overwhelmingly of Turkish background (2.2 million out of the more than 3 million Muslims), is divided into many groups with various approaches to religious instruction and practice. It has been difficult to devise a unified curriculum and for the educational authorities to know with whom to negotiate. The response has been, in many cases, to offer a form of instruction that is based less on the "Sunday school model" of religious instruction that prevails for the Christian faiths, and more on a comparative religion model in which the student is taught aspects of the Islamic faith from a more "neutral" or academic point of view (Fetzer and Soper 2005:112). Thus, while the provision of religious instruction in the schools offers Muslim residents possible future opportunities to pursue their goals, at the moment these opportunities have generally not been extended to them (Fetzer and Soper 2005).

Participants in the Gülen movement and leaders and staff of the learning centers have generally played a low-key role in the often emotionally charged policy debate concerning religious instruction in schools. As the Director of the Intercultural Center in Munich put it, he offers his opinion only when asked by the relevant officials (Interview 1). While some groups advocate the teaching of Islam in the Turkish language, he insists that Islam must be taught in German by instructors trained within the system of state schools. Previously, some religious instruction has been offered through Turkish mother-tongue classes in co-operation with the Turkish government, which has provided the curriculum as well as the teachers. Islamic instruction in Turkish—which in the view of more than one observer "sometimes seems to be more nationalist than religious"—is part of the classes (Rohe 2004:95). More recently, states have been experimenting with classes in religious instruction in which the content of the class is determined through Round Table discussions with local Muslim groups. Several universities, such as the University of Erlangen-Nuremberg, have also established programs for training teachers of Islamic religious instruction (Rohe 2004:96–97).

These kinds of programs appear to be supported by Gülen movement participants, who see Islamic religious instruction by German-trained, German-speaking teachers as meeting with the best success in the schools. This does not mean, however, that they do not see a role for themselves in providing ethical training in their centers and schools. While they eschew any formal religious instruction in classes, Gülen-inspired learning centers are centered upon providing ethical training to students in which the Qur'an can offer a clear reference point and guide. In some centers, such motivational or ethical education classes are required; in others they are optional.[1] The Director of the Bodensee Learning Center in Munich made a clear distinction between the education and learning missions of his center. While education focuses on improving the students' performance in a particular subject, learning is concerned with ethical and cultural questions. He is quick to point out that the Learning Center does not offer courses on the Qur'an or on prayer; that is the job of the mosque. Education at his center does, however, focus on the right way to live, on proper relations with others, and on moral and ethical actions. In this sense, he argued, it is impossible to leave out reference to the Qur'an. As he put it, "when we refer to German law, we are not lawyers nor are we engaged in teaching the law. Nevertheless, the law is essential for understanding proper public behavior. The same is true with the Qur'an. Of course we refer to it when it is relevant" (Interview 2). This emphasis on ethical training involves not only an Islamic reference point, it also focuses on conveying "traditional Turkish values," above all, a respect for one's parents and other authority figures and an emphasis on the importance of family.

An essential component of this ethical training necessarily involves relations with the larger German society and, by implication, a particular vision of integration. That vision is based on highlighting the student's Turkish cultural roots while at the same time emphasizing the need to "live comfortably in the culture in which one finds oneself" (Interview 7). According to the Director of the Bodensee Learning Center, the main emphasis of the learning component of the school should be on teaching these children their Turkish culture and heritage. According to him, students rarely need to be taught more about German culture since they live in the midst of it, but often they know far less about their own culture. Thus, they should be taught more about Turkish culture and values, and then they can synthesize the two. Traditional Turkish values can also help them to solve the problems they encounter in everyday life in Germany (Interview 2).

The Director of the Learning Center in Wedding, Berlin approached this question in a slightly different manner. Students at this center attend

---

[1] For example, at the Atlantic Learning Center in Ingolstadt, students typically enroll in eight hours of instruction per week, with an additional optional two hours in a "motivation course." The Director estimated that over fifty percent of the students choose to attend the motivational course.

weekly "motivational groups" that deal with relational and life issues. A strong theme of these groups is the need to get along with others, especially the Germans with whom they come into contact every day, and to avoid physical aggression in interactions with them. He told a story of a boy in the 7th grade who listened to this message in motivational class week after week and finally, one day, he had had more than he could stand. "But how?" he asked. "We want to be friends with the Germans but they don't want to be friends with us. They tease us, and insult us and bully us. What are we supposed to do about that?" Such situations are not uncommon, this director said, and they try to help students find a way to respond to them that does not involve using their fists (Interview 3).

In addition to helping students respond to the tensions arising in school between the Turkish and German students, learning centers also attempt to reach the parents and to exert a positive influence on the tensions relating to integration that arise within the family. Parents are required to attend parent sessions at the centers at least once monthly, where they are provided with guidance about how best to help their children academically. But these sessions and the frequent visits to the home by the center's teaching staff address the deeper questions of parent–child relations. Many of these parents come from rural, conservative backgrounds and are ill-equipped to deal with the realities of German, secular, urban life. Teachers from the learning centers attempt to navigate between the cultural clash that often arises between students and their parents over such issues as religious observance, German social norms, and interaction between the sexes.

This clash was aptly described by a Turkish woman who moved to Germany from Turkey when she was twelve. In an interview as part of a study conducted by the German sociologist, Hiltrud Schröter, she describes how difficult it was to adapt to German culture and attend school. At first, she worried that she would be academically behind her friends in Turkey because she started back two grade levels. Later, she worried that she would never catch up in Germany. Finally, just when she began to do well and to feel more at home in her new country, her parents became much stricter with her. They wouldn't let her do the things that "normal" girls her age in Germany did—go out with friends, socialize with boys, spend the night at girl friends' houses. While her parents had been relatively relaxed about social interactions in Turkey, she had the impression that they had gotten much stricter and more fearful in Germany. They seemed very concerned about

63

what others in the Turkish community would think of them and the behavior of their daughter. Her father tried "to be her friend" and explain why he wasn't allowing her to do everything she wished, but she began to lie more and more to her parents. They tried to negotiate rules—she would only go out with friends once a week or spend the night at a girl friend's house every two weeks. But it just didn't work. When she was nineteen, she packed her bags and moved out (Schröter 2003:49–62).

It is precisely these kinds of situations that may prompt parents to send their children to a learning center, not only for the academic help, but also for the help in conveying particular cultural or ethical messages. These centers may be particularly able to provide reassurance to the parents because of their religious orientation and emphasis on Turkish roots and culture at the same time that their staff are able to speak the language of modern university-educated students. The teachers interact intensively with parents and students and provide a particular model of integration to both. Indeed, teachers from the learning centers also help parents negotiate the bureaucracy at the public schools and relations with their children's teachers (Interview 2). In any case, a main goal for all the centers I visited is to help students find a way to live comfortably and productively in German society; education of students and parents alike is essential for such integration.

Establishment of Private Schools

A second controversial issue relating to Turkish integration and the educational system has to do with the establishment of private schools. In contrast to England and France, where a relatively high percentage of students are educated in private schools, only about four percent of German children attend private schools (Fetzer and Soper 2005:116). Thus, although article 7, section 4 of the German Basic Law established the right to operate private schools, the issue of opening Muslim private schools has remained much less central for the Turkish population of Germany than for the Muslim residents of France and Great Britain. The state governments of Bavaria and Berlin approved the establishment of two Muslim elementary schools in the 1980s to offer instruction in German and Arabic. Nevertheless, virtually all Turkish students continued to receive their education in public schools where they also continued to suffer from problems with performance, low levels of matriculation at the college-preparatory high schools, and high drop-out rates at the vocational high schools.

A recent study of the performance of Berlin students on the new 10th grade math exam illustrates the continued problems Turkish students face. While
96 percent of the students at college-preparatory high schools passed the exam, only 42 percent of those in vocational high schools, which have a much higher percentage of immigrant students, did so. Similarly, the results of the exam broken down by neighborhood indicate that the two areas of the city with the highest proportion of Turkish residents scored worst overall.[2] An official in charge of education described this outcome as "unsatisfactory" in that barely two thirds of the Turkish students managed to "cross this hurdle" and pass the exam (*Tages Spiegel* 2006:7). Another telling statistic is that in Berlin 20 percent of those matriculating in first grade are of Turkish background. However, only eight percent of those taking the 10th grade math exam were of Turkish background. The vast majority of Turkish students leave school only with a Vocational Certificate or without any certificate of completion at all (*Tages Spiegel* 2006:7). Currently, children with an immigration background are three times more likely to leave school without a certificate than children of German origin. According to the most recent PISA study—the OECD's comparative analysis of primary and secondary education—young people from immigrant backgrounds are significantly less likely to attend a university-track high school in Germany than those of German background. In other words, they have trouble even getting as far as university. Currently, there are only 26,000 Turkish students at German universities or roughly three percent of the university population (Dowling 2006).

In response to this situation and in keeping with its strong emphasis on education, the establishment of private schools has been a goal of the movement in Germany. After several years of attempting to convince the authorities of both the need for private Turkish schools and the ability of the Gülen movement participants to operate them, permission was granted to establish private, college-preparatory high schools in Berlin, Stuttgart, and

---

[2] Neukolm, 78% and Kreuzberg, 77%, compared to Steglitz-Zelendorf at 89%.

Dortmund. Feasibility studies for new high schools projects in other cities are currently underway.

The factors that finally caused the authorities to approve the establishment of these schools are varied. In the estimation of the Director of the Intercultural Center of Munich, it was first and foremost a matter of time. The movement has really only been active in Germany for about ten years; it has taken this length of time for its participants to establish credibility with the government and for the government to take seriously their request to establish private schools. Moreover, German-born and -educated professionals of Turkish background were able to lobby the government and to present a different picture of Turkish residents than the uneducated, working class stereotype that many officials seemed to possess. A critical part of the effort to persuade government officials appears to have been the decision to take some of them to Turkey, where they could observe first-hand the workings of the Gülen movement schools there (Interview 1). A final reason for the recent change of heart on the part of the state governments was offered by the Director of the Wedding Learning Center. According to him, the authorities finally overcame their skepticism when they saw that establishing private high schools could work to their advantage as a useful method of promoting integration. He pointed out that they are looking for groups that offer a "middle way" toward integration, and may believe that this group offers such a way (Interview 3).

The process of negotiating with the local authorities concerning the establishment and operation of learning centers and schools is necessarily one that occupies the attention of the parents and other individuals involved. Good relations with the local authorities are crucial. The directors of the learning and intercultural centers as well as the Berlin school described their relationship in a variety of ways. The Director of Atlantic Learning Center in Ingolstadt, a medium-size city of 120,000, described his relationship with local authorities in glowing terms. The mayor of the town regularly attends events sponsored by the learning center, for example celebrating Ramadan, and the Director is frequently contacted by relevant governmental agencies concerning matters relating to the center (Interview 7). For the Director of the Bodensee Learning Center, the problem has been one of access. While he had a close and cooperative working relationship with the authorities in the city of Augsburg, he found such a relationship difficult to establish in the much larger city of Munich (Interview 2). The Berlin-based TUDESB

Association, in contrast, appeared to have received rather warmer attention from the Berlin city government (Interview 3). In March of 2006, the Wedding Learning Center was visited by the Mayor of Mitte-Wedding who expressed his interest in the center's methods for teaching German to Turkish immigrants; he also asked what support his office could give them in their efforts to do so. The TUDESB Association, in its more than ten years of existence, has become increasingly adept at dealing with city authorities as its success at establishing the first, private Turkish school in Germany testifies. The people with whom I spoke indicated that at least part of this success was due to the fact that members of the Turkish community have now joined the ranks of the academic and policy-making elite. In this case the efforts of Dr. Mahmut Saygılı, a well-respected Turkish academic, were crucial in drawing up the plan of instruction for the proposed school and presenting it to city authorities, along with other representatives of the TUDESB Association (Interviews 3, 4 and 5).

The most important question facing those attempting to establish the TUDESB high school was why a separate, private school was necessary or desirable. The simple answer to that question, according to the head of the TUDESB Parent's Association, is that German schools are currently failing their large Turkish population. Many parents see this first and foremost as the fault of the German teachers who have low expectations for Turkish students and always assume the worst about their behavior. These students then internalize these poor expectations and they eventually do poorly. Unlike the previous two generations of immigrant Turks, this generation of German-born Turks doesn't have the feeling that their homeland is elsewhere. Rather, they feel like second-class citizens in their own homeland (Interview 5). Language is certainly at the root of the problem for most Turkish students. As a teacher at the Wedding Learning Center put it, most of them know German and Turkish "three quarters," while very few have mastered either one or the other. Not only does this language deficiency hinder Turkish students' ability to master the material, but the fact that 50 percent of their grade is based on oral exams causes them additional problems (Interview 6).

TUDESB High School in Berlin is intended to remedy the problems experienced by this generation of Turks resident in Germany by offering a demanding curriculum taught with an eye to their particular needs and problems. While some officials have begun to call for a reduction in admissions requirements at the university for Turkish students, parents and staff at the TUDESB High School generally appear to reject this approach (Interviews 3, 4 and 5). Rather, they insist that their high school must have more rigorous academic standards; only such outstanding academic training could justify the tuition payments required in a culture unused to private, tuition-based education (Interview 4). Moreover, the school must do a better job at bridging the gap between the Turkish parents and the largely German teaching staff than ordinary public schools. For this reason, a representative of the parent's association was hired full-time to communicate closely with parents nd teachers alike about the cultural needs and assumptions of the respective groups. Not only does this representative know all of the families personally and visit them frequently, as a trained teacher himself he is well equipped to explain the educational standards and processes of the German educational system as well as the best manner in which the parents can support their children's academic performance.

The goal upon graduation for the vast majority of these students and their parents is a place at a Germany university and a successful professional career.

While an emphasis on Turkish culture and language is an important goal of the school, instruction in religion is not. Although Berlin law currently provides for some form of Islamic religious instruction in the public schools, the TUDESB gymnasium in Berlin does not offer such a course. Instead, school authorities opted for a more general ethics course, which will be offered for the first time in the fall of 2006. This course in comparative religion will highlight the similarities in all the world's great religions as well as the importance of learning from one another (Interview 4). Such an approach is intended to dovetail with the school's general emphasis on intercultural interaction and understanding. This past year the school was chosen by the European Union as a participant in its Comenius Project, which offers intensive exchanges among schools from five countries: Poland, Bulgaria, Turkey, France, and Germany (*Tuebest* 2006).

Integration for this school, as for other Gülen-related centers, is a two-way process. Turkish culture is to be acknowledged and celebrated within the curricular framework of the German educational system and considerable energy expended in helping the German staff understand their largely Turkish clientele. According to the representative of the parents' association, this approach has begun to pay off. German teachers are expressing an increasing interest in learning about Turkish culture and two of them have begun Turkish language instruction. Moreover, the number of Turkish faculty has been steadily increasing since the establishment of the school two years ago; while the only Turkish member of the teaching staff in its first year was the Turkish language instructor, next year the school will have added two more teachers of Turkish background. In short, according to those involved with the school, integration must first and foremost involve appreciating the culture in which one lives, in this case Germany; but it does not require giving up who one fundamentally is. It is this philosophy of integration that the newly established private schools such as the TUDESB High School of Berlin are attempting to convey.

The Headscarf Dispute and Educational Policy

A final, highly contested area of educational policy concerns the issue of headscarves in the classroom. This has been a particular area of concern all over Europe, and Germany is no exception. Muslim women have been made a symbol of all that is ostensibly incompatible between "eastern, Muslim" culture and the west. In the words of one observer "the headscarf has become the symbol of a cultural conflict about the position of women in society" (Rohe 2004:93). While under the German Basic Law's freedom of religious expression clause (article 4, sections 1 and 2), German students may wear headscarves in the classroom, the situation concerning teachers has been much more complex. Since teachers are representatives of the state, and the state is constitutionally bound to maintain its neutrality in matters of religion, the state officials in Germany have generally ruled that teachers may not receive certification or receive permission to teach at state schools if they choose to wear a headscarf.

The case that set off what is referred to in Germany as "the headscarf dispute" began in 1998. Fereshta Ludin, the daughter of the ex-ambassador to Afghanistan, whose family was granted refugee status and who later gained citizenship through marriage, had wanted to be a teacher since she was thirteen when she also decided that she would wear a headscarf. The trouble began when she wanted to begin her student teaching and was told that it was not acceptable for her to wear her headscarf into the classroom. After petitioning the Minister of Culture in Bavaria, and being accepted into another School of Education in a different town, Ms. Ludin continued her teacher training. Nevertheless, when it was time for her to take her state certification examination, she was denied certification. This time the Ministry of Culture ruled that she "was not suitable to become a classroom instructor" as long as she was wearing a scarf (Oestreich 2004:37). The ruling determined that the headscarf was not necessary for religious observance, since most Muslim women do not wear it, but was rather a matter of personal expression. As such, the state was not required to extend protection to headscarf wearing under the freedom of religious expression guaranteed under the constitution. Moreover, and not quite consistently, the decision argued that headscarf-wearing teachers might exert pressure on female students to wear a headscarf "and in this way to separate themselves culturally" (Oestreich 2004:37). Thus, it was not in the interests of the state to allow teachers to wear headscarves in the classroom.

The outcome of this case met with various reactions. While some applauded the Minister for refusing to buckle under pressure from strongly religious women, others argued that she had missed an opportunity to show that not all women wearing headscarves were doing so under pressure. Discussion of Muslim dress and its significance exploded onto the public and legal stages, as many other cases began to make their way through the courts. Nevertheless, as one legal expert points out, the issue is not fundamentally a legal one, but one that involves deeper issues of cultural integration. "In my opinion, the true solution of this problem is not to be found within the sphere of law. As long as the headscarf is regarded as an instrument of suppression of women and of religious fundamentalism contrary to the values of the German democratic and humanitarian legal order by large parts of German society as whole, including a considerable number of Muslims, the problem will last" (Rohe 2004:100).

What is the role of education, as conducted by the Gülen movement in its centers and schools, in addressing the problems and challenges faced by Turkish women and girls? How can "the headscarf disputes" best be brought to a satisfactory conclusion, one that fosters the integration of the Turkish population in Germany? This is a subject that I intend to research in greater depth, but I will offer a few preliminary observations here. First, it is important to note the very high level of female activism; by some estimates up to 50 percent of the Gülen movement participants both in Germany and in Turkey are women. The efforts by these female participants "to explain to their German friends," as one interviewee put it, as well as to the public the reasons they have chosen wearing a headscarf as a form of religious observance can go a long way toward dispelling the "cultural clash" such dress currently symbolizes. As one observer put it, the fact that Germany has become such a secular society means that the public may be shocked not so much by the treatment of women as by public religious expression itself (Rohe 2004). The more that women who choose this form of religious observance can make clear to non-Muslims the difference between religious expression and cultural repression, the greater the chance for integration.

Second, the Gülen movement will most likely continue to avoid direct controversy and will eschew a highly visible role in the current struggle over permitting teachers to wear the headscarf in the classroom; such a stance is in keeping with the general goal of the organization to avoid highly charged political battles that could detract from its educational mission. At the moment, however, involvement in this controversy, at least in the private TUDESB High School, has been avoided only because there are currently no female teachers who have expressed a desire to wear the headscarf in the classroom. Nevertheless, a request to do so appears to be only a matter of time as these schools add more Turkish teaching staff. (The restrictions on headscarf wearing do not apply to the learning centers, and roughly one third of the female teachers of the centers I visited wear headscarves while they teach.) Meanwhile, the approach of the Gülen movement schools appears to be to walk a fine line between offering a model of education and integration based on the Turkish experience and culture while avoiding debates over emotionally charged issues, such as the role of women.[3]

Third, given their educational mission, it would appear that Gülen-inspired schools and centers have an excellent opportunity to tackle some of the difficult problems faced by Turkish women and girls. Since the majority of teachers at the Learning Centers are female, and in some centers, the majority of students, these are excellent settings to take steps to discourage cultural practices that result in the oppression of women. The existence of a large number of female teachers already sets an example, as do programs such as the Girls' Day celebration in the Berlin TUDESB High School, but more can be done. Cultural practices that threaten the rights of women and

---

[3] When I asked the representative of the parents' association about the eventuality of such a situation and the current laws in Berlin, he answered that when such a situation arose, they would have to inform themselves about the current Berlin laws concerning the wearing of headscarves in private schools; it is currently forbidden in public schools.

71

girls can be resisted in the context of the ethical learning or motivation programs of the centers and schools. Similarly, women can be encouraged to play leadership roles in the movement and its institutions. At the moment, there is a noticeable lack of women in leadership positions such as directors of the learning centers and representatives of the parent associations, as well as a lack of programs in the centers and schools designed to address issues of gender equality. The Gülen movement in Germany is well positioned through its educational and other institutions to lead the way in demonstrating that maintaining Turkish-Muslim identity can be compatible with gender and human rights. In so doing, it will be taking a huge step toward the integration of the Turkish minority into European society while maintaining its cultural and religious roots.

Conclusion

The issue of the integration of the Turkish community into German society has grown in importance since the events of 9/11 and the ensuing "war on terrorism." There are two, perhaps contradictory, forces presently at work in Germany concerning its large, mainly Turkish, Muslim population. On the one hand, there is a growing fear of the Muslim community in Germany. On the other, there is a sense that integration must be tackled seriously and approached differently than it has been thus far. The Gülen movement is currently attempting to pick its way carefully between these two forces in promoting its vision of integration.

The vision of integration embraced by participants of the movement is based first and foremost on education. In the past decade, the Gülen movement in Germany has been building an educational infrastructure that aims to improve the socio-economic situation of residents of Turkish background and promote their integration into German society. With hundreds of learning centers, cultural centers and schools operating throughout the country, it has attempted to put its ideals of "dialogue, education, and social engagement" into practice. Since much of the debate concerning integration revolves around educational policy, the work of these educational centers has been having a quiet but significant effect.

The education offered in these learning institutions is two-pronged. First, it is designed to provide educational support to Turkish students enrolled in German schools in all the major subjects, especially in German language. This support extends to the parents, who are coached not only on how to best promote their children's schooling, but also on difficult situations arising from the "cultural divide" that sometimes appears between them and their children. Establishing private schools will undoubtedly become increasingly important in the future, as the movement attempts to adapt its successful model of private education in Turkey to conditions in Germany. Whether viewed as a kind of transitional measure or a more permanent fixture, the goal of Gülen movement schools is the same: to promote the educational success of Turkish students through preparing them to enter the university and achieve professional success.

The second aspect of education offered by Gülen movement schools and centers involves the German population. A goal of the learning centers and schools, and especially the intercultural centers, is to promote a better understanding of the richness of Turkish culture, religion and language. The centers engage in outreach work in the community by offering Turkish language courses, organizing trips to Turkey, hosting Round Tables on topics relating to Islam and Turkish history and culture, inviting Germans to dinner at Turkish homes, including local officials in religious celebrations and other events. This educational work is intended to convey a vision of integration that is based on a two-way exchange of cultural understanding, and to counteract the cultural stereotypes about Turks held by many Germans. Such attitudes are increasingly difficult for many in the Turkish community to tolerate, especially the second and third generations of German-born Turks who feel like second-class citizens in their German homeland.

Thus, the vision of integration promoted by the Gülen movement centers is one of cultural exchange and enrichment rather than assimilation. Despite the denials of some German officials that there are Turkish ghettos in Germany many, if not most, Turks live a good portion of their lives separately from native Germans. Gülen movement centers are attempting to build a bridge between the two communities. But, the directors and teachers with whom I spoke insist that this cannot be done through assimilation. Such an approach would not work and is humiliating to the minority population. The Director of the Intercultural Center in Munich and others used the image of "Noah's pudding" to describe the process of integration they endorse. This pudding is composed of many ingredients that, while they enhance the flavor of the pudding, do not lose their distinctiveness since they are not ground together (Interview 1). Germans cannot simply hope that Turks will look exactly like they do in the end. Integration also means willingness on the part of the host population to understand and accept the values and experiences of the Turkish minority.

The Gülen movement is composed of a cadre of well-educated men and women, adept at operating in German society and able to represent the interests of the Turkish population in Germany. Gülen movement participants in Germany have avoided controversial political activities (and contact with other Turkish groups who engage in them), and have focused on providing education and cultural understanding. While Islam can be a component of this education, it is presented within the framework of Turkish culture and history. Gülen movement participants emphasize that this culture and history offer a more cosmopolitan, tolerant, and moderate form of Islam than many current models. It is this vision of a middle way that they hope can foster the integration of the Muslim population in Germany.

Interviews

Interview 1:   Isa Güzel, Director of the Interkulturelles Dialogzentrum, Munich

Interview 2:   Mehmet Kervan , Director of Bodensee Bildungscenter

Interview 3:   Serdar Amecidağ, Director of the Wedding Buildungszentrum

Interview 4:   Yusuf Şeker, physics teacher and Head of the Parents' Association of the TUDESB- Privatgymnasium in Berlin

Interview 5:   Anonymous, parent of TUDESB Privatgymnasium student, active member of TUDESB

Interview 6:   H. Hümeyra Olçes, teacher at the Wedding Bildungszentrum

Interview 7:   Mehmet Pekince, Director of the Atlantik Schulungs und Bildungscenter, Ingolstadt

Fethullah Gülen, Religions, Globalization and Dialogue

Paul Weller

This essay aims to bring Fethullah Gülen's thought on religion, globalization and dialogue into the consciousness of a more general public beyond Gülen's original "civilizational constituency" in Turkey and the Muslim world. It does so by examining Gülen's thought in relation to a number of key themes of relevance to religions, globalization, and dialogue and provides an alternative view for an "other than Muslim" and "other than Turkish" general public who know relatively little about Muslims or Islam and perceive of them only, or mainly, in terms of traditional obscurantism, modern "fundamentalism" and "Islamism," or else by association with terrorism. It also argues that Gülen's thought is of particular relevance to Muslims more generally as, in the diverse national and social contexts of their global faith community, they wrestle with the challenges of how to be faithful to Islam in a world that is both changing and has to be shared with neighbors of other religious traditions and none.

Fethullah Gülen's Biographical Context

In many ways Fethullah Gülen (1941-) can be seen as a product of the civilizational "East," having been born in Turkey, and having been formed by Islam in such a way that it has been a constant and fixed point of reference for his own personal life, his interpretation of the world, his teaching and his actions. Gülen is, however, not only an individual. Rather, in his life as well as his teaching, he is the inspirational figure for an emerging movement that

75

originally took shape in the Turkey of the late 20th century but is now found throughout many parts of the world.

Having emerged from a traditional background of training in religion, Gülen sought to make a connection between the inheritance of Islam, as it has developed in the Turkish cultural context, and the modern, "westernized" and globalized world. As Ergene (Gülen 2004d:viii) explains: "Gülen's model is…the essence of the synthesis created by the coming together of Turkish culture with Islam" and is especially a development of the Sufi tradition in which Gülen "re-generates this tolerant interpretation and understanding of Muslim-Turkish Sufism within contemporary circumstances, albeit highlighting a broader, more active, and more socially oriented vision. …Gülen opens up this framework and vision to all societies in the world, transforming and broadening it."

Gülen's teaching has particularly aimed at encouraging the younger generation to aspire to a combination of intellectual engagement and spiritual wisdom, and to give expression to this combination through concrete commitments in the service of humanity. As a result of this approach, the movement that is associated with him has invested heavily in the development of educational institutions in Turkey itself as well as, particularly but not only in the Central Asian regions of the former Soviet Union (Agai 2003).

Since retiring from formal teaching duties, much of Gülen's effort has been concentrated on establishing dialogue among the various ideologies, cultures, religions, and ethnic groups of Turkey, and of the wider world. In addition, while Gülen's thought is rooted in a strongly religious vision of the world, and his efforts for dialogue have engaged with a range of people of different religious traditions, his commitment to dialogue has extended beyond traditional religious circles alone. Thus, he also played a leading role in the establishment in Turkey in 1994 of The Journalists and Writers Foundation, a forum of which he is the Honorary President and which works for the promotion of tolerance and dialogue in a way that seeks active involvement from across all sectors of Turkish society, including people who understand themselves in secular terms. The significance of this needs to be understood against the specifically Turkish background for the relationship between religion and the secular in public life (Yavuz and Esposito 2003b:xiii-xxxiii).

Since Gülen is still alive, no biography of him has yet been produced that can have the benefit of a full retrospective on his life and work, or of the diversity of views concerning him. It is undoubtedly the case that Gülen is held in great esteem by those associated with him, as evidenced by the honorific title of *hocaefendi* (esteemed teacher) accorded to him by those who follow his teachings. But he is also a figure around whom there has been a divergence of views and also some controversy. Thus, Gülen spent some months in custody when, during the period of Turkish military rule that began in 1971, he was arrested but never indicted for organizing summer camps to disseminate Islamic ideas—something which, at that time, was viewed by the Turkish military as clandestine religious activity. In the early 1980s, a further case was prepared against Gülen by the police, but in the end he was not arrested. By the time of the premiership of Turgut Özal (Prime Minister, 1983–1989 and President, 1989–2003), Gülen was able to live and work relatively freely.

However, in the late 1990s, controversy erupted around him when a private Turkish television channel broadcast videotapes in which he was apparently seen to be preaching struggle against the secular republic and for the need to overthrow and to replace it with an Islamic state. Some of his supporters have argued that these videotapes were created from a montage of images and sound recordings sophisticatedly doctored in order to denigrate and attack him. Prosecution charges were brought against him in 2000 a few months after he had left Turkey for health reason and moved to the United States of America, where he still is today. In 2003, his trial in Turkey was postponed, subject to it being reactivated if he were to be indicted with a similar crime in the following five years. However, in 2006 he was acquitted of all charges.

The conflictual responses to Gülen and his work are reflected in the article on him and on the movement associated with him that are posted in the on-line encyclopedia, Wikipedia,[1] which includes a range of special notes on these (and other) articles.[2] The summary of the Wikipedia article on Gülen

---

[1] Wikipedia, the on-line encyclopedia, is described on its home page (http://en.wikipedia.org/wiki/Main_Page, retrieved on August 14, 2006) as "the free encyclopaedia that anyone can edit."

[2] In the article on "the Gülen movement" there is a note that says: "The neutrality of this article is disputed." Wikipedia has a policy referred to as 'NPOV' or 'neutral point of view',

himself perhaps best reflects the kind of positions that many have taken up with regard to him, namely that: "His supporters hail him as an important Islamic scholar with liberal ideas, while detractors accuse him for illegal activities aimed at undermining the secular republic and replacing it with an Islamic state."

Gülen, Globalization, Islam, Turkey, and Toynbee

On the level of ideas, Gülen evidences thought and imagination on a scale far wider than many in the cultural and religious traditions in which he was brought up. In so doing, he has challenged some of the general expectations of his inherited civilizational contexts. In particular, Gülen has stood out against the dichotomous and restricted options seemingly available to Muslims in the contemporary "westernized" and globalized world.

The significance of this can be seen against the background of the analysis of the relations between Islam and the West that were sketched by the British historian Arnold J. Toynbee in what was, in many ways, a prescient essay, published in 1948, "Islam, the West and the Future." Although during the First World War, Toynbee had a personal and professional history that might not seem to presage any sympathy with either Turks, Turkey, or Islam, his early publications need to be understood in the context of the War, and also in relation to the perspectives that, from looking out upon the world as a product of the heyday of the British Empire, it was almost inevitable that he would hold early in his career. [3]

---

and outlined at http://en.wikipedia.org/wiki/Wikipedia:Neutral_point_of_view (retrieved on August 14, 2006).

[3] During the First World War Toynbee (1915) wrote reports that informed the influential pamphlet that appeared with a preface by Viscount Bryce, under the title of the Armenian Atrocities: The Murder of a Nation. This was followed by a pamphlet under Toynbee's (1917) name, and entitled The Murderous Tyranny of the Turks. Toynbee's biographer, William McNeill, explains of this phase that, "Later, Toynbee came to feel that this lopsidedness was a betrayal of historical truth. His sympathies, in fact, reversed themselves, partly because he felt he had been unjust to the Turks and needed to make atonement." (McNeill 1989:74). Toynbee's other publications on Islam and Turkey eventually became quite extensive. Full details can be found in F. Morton. (1980). A Bibliography of Arnold J. Toynbee. London: Oxford University Press.

However, as Toynbee's career developed, he became one of the earliest people in the modern West to see history in a truly global rather than a Western perspective alone.[4] Thus, asked in a 1965 NBC programme about how he would like to be remembered, Toynbee (McNeill 1989:284) said, "As someone who has tried to see it whole, and...not just in western terms." Toynbee (1948:184) identified the fact that: "Islam and our Western society have acted and reacted upon one another several times in succession, in different situations and in alternating roles." In relation to Islam, he (1948:187) argued that there were "two alternative ways open to it of responding to the challenge" of the emerging global and "westernizing" world of the post–Second World War context.

Toynbee characterized these alternatives by reference typologies of response and challenge that were derived from Jewish history in the Greco-Roman era, and which he called the responses of either the Zealot or the Herodian. The way in which Toynbee describes these two possible responses remains of illuminative value today, both with regard to Gülen's teaching and the movement associated with this, as well as for the situation of Islam in Turkey and, indeed, for the general situation of Islam in the contemporary world.

Of the Zealot, Toynbee (1948:188) says that he is one who "takes refuge from the unknown in the familiar." The Herodian he (Toynbee 1948:193) describes as one who "acts on the principle that the most effective way to guard against   the danger of the unknown is to master its secret." As compared to Zealotry, Toynbee (1948: 195) sees Herodianism as "an incomparably more effective form of response...to the inexorable 'Western

---

[4] By the early 1920s he was developing a more independent view which argued for the importance of recognizing the emerging currents of Islamic self-determination. This was reflected in Volume I of the third of his annual Chatham House Survey of International Affairs that appeared under the title of The Islamic World Since the Peace Settlement (Toynbee 1925), while his 1922 book, The Western Question in Greece and Turkey: A Study in the Contact of Civilizations reversed the traditional "Western" formulation of issues referred to as the "eastern question." This latter approach, in turn, presaged what ultimately became Toynbee's multi-volume magnum opus, A Study of History (Toynbee 1934a, 1934b, 1934c, 1939a, 1939b, 1939c, 1954a, 1954b, 1954c, 1954d, with two further volumes in 1958 and 1961), which attempted to create a universal history of civilizations that was not limited by Western perspectives alone.

question' that confronts the whole contemporary world," but he also notes that "it does not really offer a solution." This is because Toynbee saw Herodianism as involving a dangerous balancing act which he described as,

> a form of swapping horses while crossing a stream, and the rider who fails to find his seat in the new saddle is swept off by the current to a death as certain as that which awaits the "Zealot" when, with spear and shield, he charges a machine gun. [Toynbee 1948:195]

Toynbee, then, identified Republican Turkey as the epitome of the Herodian response:

> Here, in Turkey, is a revolution which, instead of confining itself to a single plane, like our successive economic and political and aesthetic and religious revolutions in the West, has taken place on all these planes simultaneously and has thereby convulsed the whole life of the Turkish people from the heights to the depths of social experience and activity. [Toynbee 1948:196]

Toynbee (1948:198) pointed out that the two "inherent weaknesses" of Herodianism are that it is "mimetic and not creative" and also that even success in mimesis "can bring salvation—even mere salvation in this world—only to a small minority of any community which takes the 'Herodian' path" (Toynbee 1948:199).

He then went on to summarize the paradoxical situation that arises from the pressure to choose between these dichotomous alternatives, in the following way:

> The rare "Zealot" who escapes extermination becomes the fossil of a civilization which is extinct as a living force; the rather less infrequent "Herodian" who escapes submergence becomes a mimic of the living civilization to which he assimilates himself. Neither the one nor the other is in any position to make any creative contribution to this living civilization's further development. [Toynbee 1948:199]

Toynbee furthermore argued that both Herodian and Zealot responses are minority responses and commented that,

> The destiny of the majority...is neither to be exterminated nor to be fossilized nor to be assimilated, but to be submerged by being enrolled in the vast, cosmopolitan, ubiquitous proletariat which is one of the most portentous by-products of the "Westernization"

of the world.
[Toynbee 1948:201]

With the advantage of a hindsight that Toynbee did not have before he died in the 1970s, we can see that in Turkey what Toynbee called the Herodian stance has been continued by secularists, while the Zealot reaction of an Islamist political ideology has also emerged. And there is a tendency for many people in both Western and Muslim societies to want to limit the available choices to these two options.

Lerner (1958: 405), writing of the transformation of Turkish peasant life, expressed vividly the nature of such dichotomous choices when he spoke of alternatives of "Mecca or mechanization." The question of how to navigate through the insistence on these alternatives that can often found among secularists, religious traditionalists, and new Islamists alike is a central part of the challenge facing Gülen and the movement associated with him, and especially so in his homeland of Turkey.

It is arguable, though, that Gülen's teaching represents an attempt to find an alternative path as reflected in the title of Ahmet Kuru's (2003:115–130) essay "Fethullah Gülen's Search for a Middle Way Between Modernity and Muslim Tradition." Of course, steering a middle or third way is a project that is fraught with difficulty. In politics, third ways have often been viewed with a certain skepticism on the basis that, in the end, they have turned out not to have been third ways after all, but rather variants on one or other dominant ideology. There remains a possibility that this may become the fate of the movement initiated by Gülen.

At this point in time the outcome cannot definitively be known. However, what is significant and potentially creative with regard to Gülen and his teaching is that the middle way that he advocates is not a road of mere compromise but is one that is rooted in a particular understanding and application of traditional Islam and in which Islam is itself identified in terms of a middle way. As Kuru argues,

> Gülen does not try to create an eclectic or hybrid synthesis of modernity and Islam or to accommodate the hegemony of modernity by changing Islamic principles. What he does is reveal a dynamic interpretation of Islam that is both compatible with and critical of modernity and Muslim tradition. [Kuru 2003:130]

Indeed, Gülen interprets the very important Islamic concept of "the straight path" as precisely the middle way between excesses and deficiencies. He explains:

> Islam, being "the middle way" of absolute balance—balance between materialism and spiritualism, between rationalism and mysticism, between worldliness and excessive asceticism, between this world and the next—and inclusive of the ways of all the previous prophets, makes a choice according to the situation. [Gülen 1995:200–201]

Whether, during the process of translating these ideals into the kind of choices that need to be made in the midst of the ambiguities of the political and economic currents of history, it will be possible to maintain such balance in relation to the gravitational pull of the typologically Zealot or Herodian responses is a real question. And the outcome of this question may be of considerable importance for the future of Islam, and also for the potentially positive geopolitical role that Turkey, as a possible future member of the European Union, could have as a geographical, political and cultural bridge between historic civilizational zones.

With regard to Turkey's relations with the West, while adopting a tone of western superiority as a rhetorical device in order to make the point, Toynbee noted that, "while we did not like the outrageous old-fashioned Turkish 'Zealot'" and "we set ourselves to humble his pride by making his particularity odious," having "pierced his psychological armour and goaded him into that 'Herodian' revolution" in which he "searched out every means of making himself indistinguishable from the nations around him," the ironic result is that the West is "embarrassed and even inclined to be indignant" (Toynbee 1948:198)! And so, summarizing the invidious situation into which a society such as Turkey can be forced, Toynbee explained that,

> The victim of our censure might retort that, whatever he does, he cannot do right in our eyes, and he might quote against us, from our own Scriptures, "We have piped unto you and ye have not danced; we have mourned to you and ye have not wept." [Toynbee 1948:198]

Given the nature of the objections that emerged in the recent decision to initiate a timetable for Turkey's accession to the European Union, these observations made by Toynbee as long ago as 1948 would still appear to be pertinent. But looking beyond Turkey and the European Union to the broader position of Muslims in general, Toynbee also identified the possibility of a more mixed position emerging alongside the dichotomous alternatives of the Zealot or the Herodian response. In connection with this, he warned that,

> A panmixia may end in a synthesis, but it may equally well end in an explosion; and, in that disaster, Islam might have a quite different part to play as the active ingredient in some violent reaction of the cosmopolitan underworld against its Western masters. [Toynbee 1948:209]

Drawing attention to the Prophet's original liberation of Syria and Egypt from Hellenic domination, and to Islam's defense against the Crusaders and the Mongols, Toynbee (1948:212) went on to note that, "On two historic occasions in the past, Islam has been the sign in which an Oriental society has risen up victoriously against an Occidental intruder." Referring to historical precedents in which unexpected currents and movements (as in the case of Christianity) burst out from the underside of history, Toynbee (1948:203) pointed out the possibility that such precedents may "portend that Islam, in entering into the proletarian underworld of our latter-day Western civilization, may eventually compete with India and the Far East and Russia for the prize of influencing the future in ways that may pass our understanding." In summing up these futurological speculations, he (Toynbee 1948:212) warned that a world which cries out for anti-Western leadership may "have incalculable psychological effects in evoking the militant spirit of Islam…because it might awaken echoes of an heroic age."

The foresight of this speculation, written over half a century ago, can today be better appreciated given the positioning around Islam that has taken place in contemporary regional and global conflicts. Thus, Gülen has observed that,

> Islamic societies entered the twentieth century as a world of the oppressed, the wronged, and the colonized; the first half of the century was occupied with wars of liberation and independence, wars that   carried over from the nineteenth century. In all these wars, Islam assumed the role of an important factor uniting people and spurring them to action. As these wars were waged against what were seen as invaders, Islam, national independence and liberation came to mean the same thing. [Gülen 2004d:239]

In describing this historical development, Gülen both relates the factuality of what has occurred in the interaction between Muslims and the broad currents of global politics, and he also identifies the roots of a current concern that, for many, Islam has become a political ideology bringing with it damaging consequences for Islam, Muslims, and the world. Gülen explains:

> When those who have adopted Islam as a political ideology, rather than a religion in its true sense and function, review their self-proclaimed Islamic activities and attitudes, especially their political ones, they will discover that the driving force is usually personal or national anger, hostility, and similar motives. If this is the case, we must accept Islam and adopt an Islamic attitude as the fundamental starting point for action, rather than the existing oppressive situation. [Ünal and Williams 2000:248]

This is because without such a re-evaluation it remains the case that, "The present, distorted image of Islam that has resulted from its misuse, by both Muslims and non-Muslims for their own goals, scares both Muslims and non-Muslims" (Ünal and Williams 2000:248).

Indeed, in the adoption of terrorist activities and justification of them, such an ideologized version of Islam has further distorted both Islam and its image in the wider world. With regard to such activities Gülen took up a very clearly articulated position. Thus, in the wake of the 9/11 attacks, in the Washington Post newspaper of September 21, 2001, Gülen stated clearly:

> We condemn in the strongest of terms the latest terrorist attack on the United States of America, and feel the pain of the American people at the bottom of our hearts. Islam abhors acts of terror. A religion that professes "He who unjustly kills one man kills the whole of humanity," cannot condone the senseless killing of thousands. Our thoughts and prayers go out to the victims and their loved ones.

In his "Message Concerning the September 11 Terrorist Attacks" Gülen (2004d:261–262) went further to state clearly that, "Islam does not approve of terrorism in any form. Terrorism cannot be used to achieve any Islamic goal. No terrorist can be a Muslim, and no real Muslim can be a terrorist." Furthermore, in his piece entitled "Real Muslims Cannot be Terrorists," Gülen explains,

> The reasons why certain Muslim people or institutions that misunderstand Islam are becoming involved in a terrorist attacks

84

throughout the world should not be sought in Islam, but within the people themselves, in their misinterpretations and in other factors. Just as Islam is not a religion of terrorism, any Muslim who correctly understands Islam cannot be or become a terrorist. [Gülen 2004d:179]

Gülen has a realistic evaluation of the historical forces at work in the world in a way which takes account of Realpolitik while also setting this within a religious vision of historical development that challenges all current holders of power to see their own tendency to hubris and their historical relativity in the passage of time. This is presented as a general truth that encourages us to try to trace meaning in the patterns of history, but it can also be understood with specific reference to recognizing that the past hundred or so years of Western dominance are, in historical perspective, only a very small span in the course of the rise and fall of civilizations. With regard to the dominant powers of the world Gülen explains his position that,

> There has always been a power that has kept the balance in the world and there always will be. This power was once Rome; then for a time it was Islam, first with the Arabs, and then through the Muslim Turks that assumed this function. Starting with the nineteenth century, the Anglo-Saxon world has taken hold of this position of balancing the world; first it was the British Empire that did this, followed by, after World War II, America. God states in the Holy Qur'an that He gives property to whomever he wishes, and also that He takes it away from whomever he wishes. [Gülen 2004d:247]

However, while Gülen's vision of history is set within a clear theological perspective that the framework of things is ultimately determined by the will of God, he also affirms that, within this, humanity's actions and choices can bring about varied effects. Therefore, when considering the role of global power held by the USA in the contemporary world Gülen (2004d:248) reflects that, "Today, the USA engages the dominant position in the political balance of the world. However, its dominance depends on whether it continues to act on the basis of justice and human rights" and that "no system can live long if it is supported solely by force. Force that does not depend on rights and justice will inescapably diverge toward oppression and thus prepare its own end."

Informed by such a perspective, while clearly condemning the 9/11 attacks, it is significant that Gülen also warned about the kind of response that the USA might make. Expressing it in words, the force and resonance of which are only underlined by what has occurred over the past five years, Gülen said,

> Before America's leaders and people respond to this heinous assault out of their justified anger and pain, please let me express that they must understand why such a terrible event occurred and let us look to how similar tragedies can be avoided in the future. They must also be aware of the fact that injuring innocent masses in order to punish a few guilty people is to no one's benefit; rather, such actions will only strengthen the terrorists by feeding any existing resentment and by giving birth to more terrorists and more violence. [Gülen 2004d:262]

Sadly, the prescience of Gülen's warning can be seen all too clearly in the continuing instability of Afghanistan; in the quagmire of death and destruction that Iraq has become; in the tangled metal and bloody aftermath of the train bomb in Madrid in March 2004; and most recently of all in London Transport bombings of July 2005, and the second Bali bombing. In the 21st century, the opening years of which have been characterized by events of this kind, there is a need for resources that can be offered through the thinking of those who can understand and interpret the currents of history. By building on such understanding and interpretation, Gülen has become increasingly committed to affirming the possibility of and need for inter-civilizational and interreligious dialogue.

Gülen, History and Dialogue

Gülen advocates a view of history that diverges from predominant secular histories in its evaluation of the dynamic of religion as the main key for understanding civilizational change. Thus, Gülen argue:

> Regardless of changes, advancements in science and technology, and new ways of thinking, the feeling of attachment to a religion has always been the primary factor in forming humanity's scientific and intellectual life, developing human virtues, and establishing new civilizations. With its charm and power, religion is still and will continue to be the most influential element and power in people's lives. This reality will continue to exist. The existence of two great civilizations in history, one based mainly on Islam and the other owing a good deal to Christianity, proves this argument. [Ünal and Williams 2000b:43]

Toynbee (1948:87) referred to the critical importance for modern life of what he called the "annihilation of distance" that had been brought about by technology and modern means of transportation and because of which he argued "all local problems" have been converted into "world-wide problems." Gülen has also observed:

> Modern means of communication and transportation have transformed the world into a large, global village. So, those who expect that any radical changes in a country will be determined by that country alone and remain limited to it, are unaware of current realities. This time is a period of interactive relations. Nations and people are more in need of and dependent on each other, which causes closeness in mutual relations. [Gülen 2004d:230]

One of the consequences of the creation of this global village is the need to recognize that interreligious dialogue is not a luxury; it has become not only desirable but also necessary. An increasing number of Gülen's publications address the need for such dialogue. In a compact and accessible way, the main contours of Gülen's thinking on dialogue can be found in his article "The Necessity of Interfaith Dialogue: A Muslim Perspective" (Ünal and Williams 2000b:241–256) and in his piece "At the Threshold of a New Millennium" (Ünal and Williams 2000b:225–232), the texts of both of which, it should be noted, were written before the global religious and political shock of 9/11 and its aftermath, underlining that Gülen's advocacy of dialogue is not merely reactive and pragmatic, but is rooted in his vision of Islam and the contemporary world. Thus, in his millennium reflections, Gülen set out his conviction about the importance of dialogue in the following way:

> I believe and hope that the world of the new millennium will be a happier, more just and more compassionate place, contrary to the fears of some people. Islam, Christianity and Judaism all come from the same root, have almost the same essentials and are nourished from the same source. Although they have lived as rival religions for centuries, the common points between them and their shared responsibility to build a happy world for all of the creatures of God make interfaith dialogue among them necessary. This dialogue has now expanded to include the religions of Asia and other areas. The results have been positive. As mentioned above, this dialogue will develop as a necessary process, and the followers of all religions will find ways to become closer and assist each other. [Gülen 2004d:231]

Conclusions

In his writing and teaching Gülen affirms the existence of a fundamental continuity in the issues faced by human beings in relation to their behavior with one another and their place in the universe. At the same time, he recognizes the specific nature of the challenges of diversity and plurality—challenges which have previously been present in individual historical societies but which, in the 21st century, have been elevated onto a global stage. To be able to live creatively and with integrity in a world such as this without becoming trapped into the response of either Herodian compromise or Zealot reaction is challenging. As addressed to Muslims—but arguably also with potential applicability to others—Gülen (2004d:42) has explained that, "Tolerance does not mean being influenced by others or joining them; it means accepting others as they are and knowing how to get along with them."

Thus, Gülen stands against ways of thinking and acting that promote the illusion that the uncomfortable plurality of the contemporary world can simply be abolished. Against such illusions Gülen warns:

> Different beliefs, races, customs and traditions will continue to cohabit in this village. Each individual is like a unique realm unto themselves; therefore the desire for all humanity to be similar to one another is nothing more than wishing for the impossible. For this reason, the peace of this (global) village lies in respecting all these differences, considering these differences to be part of our nature and in ensuring that people appreciate these differences. Otherwise, it is unavoidable that the world will devour itself in a web of conflicts, disputes, fights, and the bloodiest of wars, thus preparing the way for its own end. [Gülen 2004d:249–250]

Gülen's thought offers intellectual and spiritual resources that enable us better to understand the one world in which we all live, as well as to engage with the challenges that living in this world brings. Such resources are needed for understanding the nature and dynamics of the world, and for enabling us to resist the kind of disastrous outcomes which some argue are inevitable, which many others fear, and which all of us have a responsibility and a possibility to do something about.

The Most Recent Reviver in the *'Ulama* Tradition: The Intellectual *'Alim*, Fethullah Gülen

Ali Bulaç

In the course of the eighteenth and nineteenth centuries the Islamic world underwent a deep crisis and two approaches emerged to offer potential solutions. One of these places emphasis on the state and politics and is committed to building a new society and political entity. The other is based upon social reform and intellectual transformation. The key words for the first perspective are politics and the state, whereas education and spiritual improvement are the key terms for the latter. In this essay they will be referred to as *State Islam* and *Civil Islam*, respectively. Both approaches have continuing influence in our day.

Fethullah Gülen is currently one of the most prominent representatives of the second line. Thus, it would be appropriate to consider him as a social reviver whose origins are in the *'ulama* tradition. This paper will draw attention to the features of Gülen's perspectives on civil space and how his efforts to raise a new, educated generation differ from other reformist or revival movements.

First, however, it is necessary to clarify the notion of Civil Society by reference to Islamic-Ottoman history, in order to define clearly pivotal concepts like *civil initiative* and *civil space* as they are manifested in the Muslim context.

Civil Society in Islam and the Ottoman Experience

The framework of civil society is shaped by religion in Islamic history; in other words, the most powerful civil space is implemented by Islam, through which religiously derived prescriptions protect the public from its administration. In connection with this, religious communities, Sufi orders, *ahi* (trade guilds with attached religious scholars), foundations, and dervish lodges have traditionally constituted the most influential, permanent, and functional civil organizations.

In many ways, the norms of these organizations continue to have a strong presence, despite radical splits.

In order to define civil society in Muslim societies accurately and draw its borderlines properly, it is useful to contrast it with two central features of the concept of civil society in the West:

1. Western civil society emerged from a group structure which was divided into classes and from a history of conflicts between these classes. In effect, civil society in the West was an endeavor by the bourgeoisie to seek a space, for they belonged not to the absolutist administration, aristocracy, church, village or town, but rather to the burgs—intermediary settlements or castles. Thus, this civil society had its very foundations laid upon class-consciousness or the class factor, whereas civil space in Islamic history does not have class-based foundations.

2. While in the process of forming such a space of its own, the worldview and persuasions of western civil society tended towards being predominantly secular. In this respect, the civil society is the product of a development that gives priority to democratic government and secularism as opposed to absolute administration and theocracy, respectively. In the Islamic world, the proponents of enlightenment adopt the West as a universal paradigm. They associate politics with liberal democracy—thought to be the apex at which capitalism has arrived. Likewise, they associate civil society with the bourgeoisie and its particular ideology.

However, contrary to what Montesquieu, Witfogel, or Marx argued, the fact that civil society has not been formulated as a concept in the Islamic world is not because there is an absolute state despotism which effectively

90

puts all societal life behind bars. In the historical experience, there have been a greater number of free and autonomous spaces in the Islamic world than the West has ever had. These spaces were not patriarchal or hierarchical to the exaggerated extent that has been claimed. Islamic societies never felt the need for a civil society similar to that of the West.

In Islamic history, civil space was necessarily defined in relation to religion, as a result of which a civil space is considered impossible without religion, even today. This is because in history, especially during the Ottoman period, the specific nature of civil space was essentially formulated by the religion itself. The Örfi Law, which corresponds to today's constitutional law, defined the administration, whose only concern was the security of the Sultan and the throne. The Ottomans arranged the administration or the political and official space by reference to the Örfi Law, leaving the organization of civil space itself to the dictates of religion—allowing the growth and sustenance of a social scope which was wide, functional, and influential. If a historical model is worth taking as a reference, then we can argue that the parameters that made the civil space possible in the past are also indicators for today, on condition that the historical public law has been democratized.

As far as civil society in Turkey in its simplest form is concerned, it is NGOs which represent the space outside the official domain that first spring to mind. Modern civil society groups or associations, which operate within the secular framework and aim to be influential over decision-making mechanisms, are alienated from society, for they are based upon a different historical and social legacy. In the final analysis, they favor the state's presumptions over the interests of society and civil initiatives, much like a trade union which always sides with the employer. Leaders of these modern civil institutions distance themselves from the public, in a way similar to that of secular intellectuals who have a self-proclaimed mission to illuminate society in the framework of Enlightenment philosophy, as they place their allegiance with the state authority, and not with the civil space. As a result, we can argue there is a serious problem of "civil representation" in Turkey and much of the Islamic world.

In contrast, Fethullah Gülen is truly a civil leader. The community which has gathered around him is carrying forward a profound historical legacy with a modern approach, and thus it is possible to talk about a natural representation within this formation.

Given this preliminary discussion, it is now possible to ask whether there is any true civil space in Turkey today. As mentioned already, in Islam, the boundaries of the state are pre-determined and confine a small space, an issue for which the consensus of the Hanafi jurists[1] provides a practical reference. The *imam* (here, head of state) enjoys four specific rights (space and authority): sovereignty and representation of sovereignty (for example, the practice of public Friday prayer); protection regarding domestic security, justice, and jurisdiction (the authority to sentence); tax collection in order to meet collective and indivisible needs and for the protection of the poor; and the defense of the country or the declaration of war. Hence, every social activity falling outside these four authorities has traditionally belonged to the civil space.

If the Muslim world is to have civil spaces, then this cannot occur if they are separated from religion or from community leaders who have taken as their basis the historical and intellectual heritage of Islam. In this regard, a powerful return of a new group of scholars and thinkers whose reference is the religious sources—not those intellectuals who expect a signal or an invitation from the government—to what is social and public, is necessary, at least at an intellectual level. The example of Fethullah Gülen indicates such attempts will prove successful.

State Islam and Civil Islam

Muslim society is currently undergoing a severe rupture, yielding profound impacts. This is especially true with respect to public perception and to the efforts to explain the projects of change which are imposed from the outside, and even more generally with regard to the conceptual framework of change itself and its inner dynamics.

The present problems are the residue of specific problems inherited from the eighteenth and nineteenth centuries. Unfortunately, not only problems and crises, but also actors, institutions, and paradigms were carried over into the twentieth century. Even today, problems are handled strictly by reference to Islam or Islamism, and solutions are sought, in the most general term, within the "facilities that Islam offers."

---

[1] Experts on jurisprudence in the Hanafi school of Islam, the majority school in Turkey.

Historically speaking, the pioneer of State Islam was Jamaladdin Afghani, while the pioneer of Civil Islam was Muhammad Abduh. Not in their references but with regards to socio-political objectives there are essential differences between these two approaches. Anyone wishing to consider the various attitudes of the Muslim actor and how he has been influenced by Islam and the spirit of the time must be aware of the significant divergence between these lines of thought; for failing to be aware of this distinction will always lead to an incorrect appraisal of the matter.

1. *State Islam.* This is a state project and a *Tanzimat* (Ottoman reform movement which started in 1834) tradition which takes political authority as its center. This design fits well into the general intellectual and political circumstances that correspond to the first emergence of the current of Islamism. The primary goal of the first Islamist generation, which took the stage in 1856–1924, was to save the Ottoman State, the founding ideology of which was Islam, and whose political format shared more or less the same denominator with other movements such as pan-Turkism, Ottomanism, and Westernism. *Dar al-Islam* (the abode in which the Ottomans exercised political and military authority) was facing a number of predicaments and it was thought that a solution could be found for these by restructuring the state to ensure its efficient operation. Reforming society was also important, but capturing the state would necessarily involve securing control over the society and institutions too, and this would facilitate the realization of social reforms within the state organization. To achieve this, the first Islamist generation adopted a top-down policy for Islamicization. Thus, State Islam, in accordance with its nature, would be based upon an official religious ideology with obscure totalitarian tendencies. The objective was to reform the world, not by "becoming Muslim" but by "making Islamic."

2. *Civil Islam.* Muhammad Abduh and many others who have followed him make it clear that Civil Islam is based on a societal project which embarks on the mental reformation of individuals. This line takes as its basis the individual's introspection into his or her religious convictions in order to make corrections, thus freeing himself or herself in the face of tradition, and actively using reason. It lays a higher importance on the society than on the state, and it is

93

motivated to achieve the general reformation of the society, not the state, for it is founded on the acceptance of diversity and is, therefore, at peace with variation. Its cultural and social identity is dominant over political and military identity. Thus, it seeks a bottom-up change which advocates "becoming Muslim." Its emphasis is on the periphery and change, rather than on the center, though it does not explicitly exclude what is political.

Civil Islam is an alternative to political or military challenges to the world, and it since it emphasizes a pluralistic worldview, it is more tolerant of different lifestyles, religions and cultures. As opposed to State Islam, Civil Islam maintains democratic participation rather than the central ideology of sovereignty, and brings politics one level down.

In conclusion, State Islam is almost like a quotation from the West's Enlightenment. According to my understanding, while the Civil Islam model has comprised the main body of Islam until the mid-Abbasid period, and it is this Civil Islam understanding which has given continuity to Islam throughout history.

Versions of State Islam

A note should be made on conceptualization: some Islamologues define certain Islamic currents which emerge to solve the problems of the Muslim world within the domain of lawful politics, as "political Islam." This is a misleading and incorrect definition. In fact, Islam cannot be said to be completely indifferent to politics or public life. Politics play an important role in both the social Muslim identity, emphasizing social reforms, and the Muslim cultural identity, exerting its influence on intellectual anxieties. However, Islamist movements which emerge simply to establish "a new (and at the same time modern) Islamic State," or "a new integrated Islamic society" and which do not tolerate different religious, ethnic, cultural, or political voices—or to put it more clearly, movements which aim to create an "Islamic nation" and seek only to implement various socio-political projects via official instruments or organs—are clearly defined as State Islam not "political Islam."

State Islam's transformation into an Islamist movement as a result of abandoning the idea of developing its own state model while claiming to seize the present state dates back to the period marked by the years 1947–1950, which also heralded the emergence of the second Islamist generation in history.

The three most important events during this period are well documented: (1) the establishment of Pakistan as an "Islamic state in national form" in 1947, the first of its kind in Islamic history; (2) the Muslim Brotherhood's undertaking of a political mission in Egypt, departing from its social-reform identity; and (3) the end of the one-party state (1923–1950) in Turkey and its joining the new Western alliance (NATO). During the same period, we witnessed the Musaddiq movement in Iran, and then the religious scholars there made an attempt to create their first political movement by revolting in Hordat in 1964. Fifteen years later, a revolution took place in Iran in February, 1979.

We experienced four versions of State Islam in the twentieth century:

1. *Revolutionary*. The Iranian Revolution and other revolutionary movements which followed its model.

2. *Insurrectionary*. The insurrection of Pakistani Ziya al-Haqq; the Muslim Brotherhood in Syria; the Hizb al-Tahrir Organization in Jordan; etc.

3. *Democratic*. The Jamaat al-Islam Party of Pakistan; the MSP-RP-FP[2] experience in Turkey; the Islamic Salvation Party of Algeria (FIS); etc.

4. *Reconciliatory*. The Muslim Brotherhood in Egypt and Jordan, who have strong direct or indirect relationships with politics; and religious communities and groups in Senegal and other countries.

It can be difficult to treat these versions in different categories because the demarcations between them are porous and allow each to have an effect on the other. Sometimes it is impossible to argue homogeneity even within one version. For instance, Said Nursi, in Turkey, defined the concept of "faith" as a transforming power and fostered the intellectual foundation of Fethullah Gülen, especially in the New Said period. However, although he was the best representative of Civil Islam, some of his followers from among

---

[2] Milli Selamet Partisi-Refah Partisi-Fazilet Partisi. One party, which changed its name several times.

the Nur communities have been steeped in the reconciliatory version of State Islam (progress by reconciliation), largely due to certain contemporary difficulties and forms of oppression. Their constructive interactions with the state do not derive from a motivation to take hold of the state, as is often alleged. On the contrary, such interactions are practiced simply to allow the movement to survive in a legitimate bureaucracy, while serving as a sort of protection within the democratic system.

The revolutionary version cannot be considered as a single category either. It comprises exceptional individuals and socio-political groups who also carry certain inclinations from the reconciliatory version.

Abul A'la Mawdudi and Sayyid Qutb are indubitably the prototype advocates of state Islam. In fact, Mawdudi was the first prototype because Sayyid Qutb developed his ideas and political view during his incarceration in Egypt after reading Mawdudi. The works of these two individuals have been very influential among those who propagate State Islam.

The debate between Jamaladdin Afghani's and Muhammad Abduh's viewpoints revived again after the 1960s. Sayyid Qutb and Malik Bennabi discussed this issue together privately. Sayyid Qutb, in Ma'alim fi-l-Tariq (Milestones), suggests that Islam is primarily "a political revolution" and "a comprehensive social change project." However, Malik Bennabi of Algeria, in *The Cause of Islam*, claims that Islam is "a civilization movement," destined to prepare for new challenges by achieving the meeting of "soil, time, and humanity" in an appropriate conjuncture.

Two Different Analyses

According to State Islam, the Islamic world is "underdeveloped" and dependent upon western industrialized countries. One way of getting over this shameful situation is to progress in the areas of science, technology and economics and reach political and military freedom. Hashemi Rafsanjani, the former President of Iran, who played an important role in helping the revolution to become institutionalized after Ayatollah Khomeini, stated that they had accomplished full political and partial cultural freedom; he went on to state that they needed to complete this freedom by developing the fields of economics and technology. They attempted to do something in this regard through construction and investment initiatives under Iran's development plans. In Turkey, the MSP (National Salvation Party), in the 1970s, preserved the idea of the national development project, emphasizing the importance of heavy industry, but otherwise they went no further than adding a secondary dimension that was called "spiritual and moral development."

State Islam proponents in Turkey emphasize a fair nationwide distribution of income; for them this is the only way to eliminate poverty and disparity between classes. This proposition, according to the RP (Welfare Party), is the "just order," which was a component of the national development model. Certainly, the unfair distribution of national income is one of the major problems in the Muslim world.

Morality for State Islam is as important as the development problem because Muslim society has experienced moral degeneration, neglected Islamic virtues, and been dragged into anarchy without solving the problem of identity and spiritual belonging. Economic recession, failing education, and the spiritual downfall and identity crisis can all be overcome by seizing the government and running it appropriately. Its modern description and mission mean that the state is a transformer as a result of its historical prestige, and financial and cultural institutions. These institutions indicate that Islam is perceived more often as a political movement than as a culture or civilization. This political movement is seen by Islamists as a way of placing politics in the centre of social life so that it rebuilds Islamic society.

Additionally, State Islam assumes that knowledge and modernism can be Islamic. From this perspective, State Islam supports development and progress. Because of these properties, although it appears skeptical about secularism, State Islam is secular and modernist—though this may seem astonishing or paradoxical. Its view of the state is inspired by the modern nation state. In this regard, State Islam is inclined to modernism, and ready and suited to open areas for modernism.

Civil Islam claims that in this way the problem is being addressed incorrectly. Because of its extreme emphasis on the state and politics, State Islam seems to be totalitarian and authoritarian. Its spiritual, ethical and intellectual dimensions are thus demoted to the dimensions of worldly politics and become one of the sites of argument about the clash of civilizations. Civil Islam is positioned at the opposite pole. First and foremost, the main problem of the Muslim world lies in the acceptance of having been defeated intellectually by the West and in its current role, despite the fact that economic phenomena do not play determinative but affective roles. The approach of "arming oneself with the enemy's weapon" for salvation makes the economy and technology absolute, and leads to new dependencies. Power should be sought not in the means of modernization but in human power and dynamics, and in society's potential energy.

Islam, according to the viewpoint of Civil Islam, is not just a state organization or a political movement; rather, it is an *umma* or community project which surpasses politics without rejecting the political dimension of life and its positive and essential effects. God's absolute will is not manifested simply within the state, but rather on a society comprised of individuals who are aware of their rights and responsibilities. A universal social project can be used as an alternative to the homogeneous universal-state of modernity. This project should shrink the state and strengthen society.

Civil Islam argues that social reform is so wide-reaching that it cannot be handled only by politics and state. The question, "Why did the Islamic world fall behind the West?" asked by Islamists so frequently since the previous century, needs to be replaced by the question, "What is Islam's answer to the modern world?" Today, historical, theoretical, and practical answers need to be found to this second question. For the first question makes us think strictly in a Cartesian, progressive, and analytical way, and leads to confusion—and a right answer can never be found for an incorrect question, or one asked wrongly. Therefore, while Muslim activists are aggressive, Muslim intellectuals are apologetic.

In the view of Civil Islam, there is great diversification today among families, Islamic civil communities, religious orders, and groups and these are all emerging as social actors, indicating that the Islamic world has a new trend parallel to globalization and urbanization. A Muslim country's problems with modernity cannot be understood without a correct understanding of this diversification. The Muslim world joins the modern period in this natural progression, and Muslims are responsible, not for the state, as in the *Tanzimat* tradition, but for society and its cultural and civil sources. Transformation will start in the intellectual, cultural, scientific, moral, and social areas. If democratic processes run properly during this period, political life will be transformed as well. However, first of all, individuals and society respectively should experience a significant intellectual change and be reinforced by means of morality. Then, we will see a society which governs itself by its own values.

Civil Islam gives priority to the Qur'an because the Qur'an was and is a source of epistemological separation from the modern west, and for regaining the power of juristic inference (*ijtihad*). Civil Islam also gives priority to the *Sunna* (Prophetic tradition), which encourages lifestyles which are a substantial alternative to those which modernism offers. Hence, Civil Islam underlines the distinctions between historical Islam, real Islam, and modernity. However, this civil approach intends neither to destroy modernity completely—overcoming it by assimilating it instead—nor to reject tradition entirely—instead rectifying it with provided trustworthy references. Just as past experiences cannot be carried over to the present day, nor can a degraded situation in the present be considered acceptable. Muslims have got to exceed modernity as well as their own history and current situations.

Questions like, "How can we become a political government?" or "How can a state be taken over?" do not make any sense in the context of Civil Islam. Rather, questions about the democratic legitimacy of a government's cultural and societal background, the democratization of the state and its institutional structure, the efficient operation of a state based on the superiority of jurisprudence, and how to make the public more influential over decision-making mechanisms are prominent today. State Islam acceded to the government from time-to-time or became a joint partner (Iran, Turkey, Pakistan, Malaysia, Jordan, Egypt, Sudan, Senegal, etc.), but this did not generate any serious improvement in the overall situation. This means that forming a government on its own or engaging in politics (as a nation state, on modern terms) is not sufficient for becoming a universal alternative.

Islamic rhetoric deals with the problems of humanity and the world; therefore, its agenda is not confined to certain national problems but rather concerned with what is universal. Islam demurs to classic modernity, as do Judaism and Christianity. This is an important point requiring a dialogue between religions stemming from the same source, and other holy and ancient traditions. Fethullah Gülen's emphasis on dialogue is, therefore, not a coincidence.

Fethullah Gülen: *Intellectual-'Ulama*

Having endured a difficult period in its modern history, the Muslim world now seems to be heading towards a new *intellectual-'ulama* period. Ernest Gellner and Serif Mardin try to understand the modern Muslim world by categorizing it as High Islam and Low Islam, but this conceptualization is erroneous. In fact, Islamic society is composed historically and intellectually of two main groups: when it comes to their intellectual capacity people are of the educated elite or scholars (*havas*) or the laypeople (*avam*). Belief, however, does not vary in Islamic society. In principle, there is no difference in belief between the educated elite and laypeople, but their speech, expression and exposition levels are different. Just as there is no difference in belief between Baki, the most distinguished person in *diwan* literature,[3] for example, and Karacaoğlan, a folk poet, or between Mawlana Jalaladdin Rumi and Yunus Emre, so there is no difference in faith, deed, vision and the understanding of the meaning of life between the elite and laypeople people of the Muslim world either. Based strictly on the differences in speech, expression and exposition, it is more appropriate to call educated Muslims *kitabi* (lettered ones) and uneducated Muslims *ummi* (unlettered ones). Of course, *ummi* does not mean ignorant; in Muslim society, there are numerous *ummi* but wise (*arif*) people.

Traditional leadership has normally been under the authority of the *'ulama*, who take *kitabi* Islam as a direct reference, or of the *murshid* (teacher), who is especially esteemed by *ummi* Islam. In the Middle East, intellectuals, who often are in organic collaboration with the central government elites, have often taken the place of the *'ulama* and the *murshid* with the support of modern states. Now, we are witnessing a new leadership profile with the blend of the two: the *intellectual-'ulama*. An *'alim* is a member of the *'ulama*, a respected religious scholar who knows the field and also practices the religion. An *'alim* is also an intellectual if he has more background knowledge than ordinary people and his perspectives are sound. Fethullah Gülen, who does not hold a university diploma from a modern university but has received a traditional training under the private tutelage of the highest scholars, is one of the most distinguished representatives of the *intellectual-'ulama* type.

---

[3] *Diwan* (also *divan*) literature: a poetic form, generally considered the highpoint of *havas* literature in the Middle East.

Intellectuals in Turkey are a product of Enlightenment philosophy, and their references are based upon the essential assumptions of the Enlightenment: rationalism, and the thought of human independence from the Transcendent. The intellectual wishes to transform society. Therefore, they are seen by the community as conservative; due to their position, they are not enlightened in the true sense of the word, and they try to transfer and enforce the arguments created by the former secular elite. Therefore, they are in disharmony with society, as well as with their culture, beliefs, and history, and as expected, they offer their allegiance to the state and politicized society.

Islamically-oriented writers in Turkey deny being intellectual, and do not like being treated as if they fall in this category because of the characteristics of the intellectual. However, they do not come from the 'ulama tradition either. They often have some kind of western education, and are engineers, economists, lawyers, sociologists, poets, writers, journalists, physicians, and so on. Their knowledge of Islamic sciences is not sufficient. They cannot easily come up with a reference from the Qur'an or the Sunna, they know almost nothing about the method of Islamic jurisprudence (*fiqh*), and their knowledge with regards to Islamic history, including theology, philosophy, Islamic thought, and Sufism does not go much beyond the textbooks.

The concept of *janahayn* (the dual wing) refers to having knowledge of both Islamic sciences and western science and education. Of the very few contenders, Gülen is perhaps the foremost representative of *janahayn*. His outlook has several key features: a profound understanding of Islamic sciences; a deep knowledge of biography (*ilm al-rijal*) in Hadith narration; and a thorough understanding of Islamic methodology (*usul*). These features are all of almost the same weight in terms of knowledge. His book, *Key Concepts in the Practice of Sufism* (originally published in Turkish as *Kalbin Zümrüt Tepeleri*), is an extremely important work in terms of thought and Sufi tradition. Gülen most important characteristic is that he analyzes contemporary issues and brings forth solutions using the traditional methodology of Islamic jurisprudence and Hadith.

If one looks at the individual profiles of those who have participated in terrorist activities recently, one will observe that the participants have generally not had a quality Islamic education and do not follow traditional Islamic methodology while attempting to issue religious rulings (*fatwa*) without being eligible to do so. Generally, they participated in Marxist or Nationalist movements during their university education and joined Islamist movements later, while retaining their tendencies towards rebellion and insurrection. In stark contrast to such people, Fethullah Gülen has the great advantage of his knowledge of Islamic methodology, the ability to give references from Islamic sciences, and knowledge of the intellectual, scientific, and artistic history of Islam. This sound methodology is a protective frame.

Thus, when making an effective sociological study of modern Turkey, it is impossible now to disregard the work of Fethullah Gülen. He has proved able to unite and mobilize large numbers of people from very many diverse backgrounds to work on significant social projects. The Gülen movement schools and other associated educational activities which he inspires around the world are also probably the most notable contribution of the nation of Turkey to global development and progress today

Personal Profile: Civil Revivalist

In recent Turkish history, the effects of social decay and disruption have also been reflected in the crisis of social leadership. The first reason for this crisis is that those who are decided on modernization have tried to assume a kind of social and cultural leadership of others. Secondly, when leaders are needed in society, they typically come from the spheres of politics or academia. However, as we have seen, society has not recognized the leadership of such self-proclaimed scholars or of those put forward in this way by the state. Therefore, the project of modernization has not been internalized by society.

In the Ottoman period, social leadership was in the hands of the '*ulama*, as in the case of traditional Muslim societies. The '*ulama*, the true leaders of society and one of the legs of the state tripod, were eliminated and replaced with an intellectual class first by the *Tanzimat* reforms, then by *Meşrutiyet* II (the second phase of constitutional monarchy from 1908) and lastly by the *Cumhuriyet* (Republic, 1923). This replacement was effected by the palace and the state during the period of the Ottomans and the Republic, respectively. The purpose was to control civil society in order to pave the way for a fully fledged process of westernization and modernization. When Mahmut II was eliminating the '*ulama*, the official '*ulama* opposed westernization in an attempt to rationalize their positions. They claimed that existing injunctions derived from religion or Islamic law did not allow such innovations and reforms. These developments caused tension between reformist authorities (military, civil bureaucrats, intellectuals) and religiously motivated scholars. In reality, Islam was not against all of these reforms, and nor were the Islamists of that time. On the contrary, starting in 1856, the first Islamists were against the oligarchy and supported the democracy.

This was an unfortunate period in Turkish history. If the official and civil *'ulama* had been supporters of the reforms, neither the palace nor the state would have become so authoritarian or totalitarian, nor would a tragic tension have emerged between society and the modern world. The palace during the period of the Ottomans, and later the state in the Republic, gave considerable care to forming an intellectual community in order to overcome the *'ulama* obstacle. The differences between the 'ulama and intellectuals can be listed as follows:

a. The references of the *'ulama* are the Qur'an, the Sunna, and traditions (Hadith); and the sources of knowledge are the Islamic sciences. In contrast, the references of intellectuals come primarily from Enlightenment thought.

b. The *'ulama* lead society in its natural progress, organize interactions in social life, and guide people for spiritual and cultural development; in contrast, intellectuals aim to transform society, so they are always in conflict with the people and their culture.

c. The *'ulama* are civil in the dominant tradition of Islam. Their power does not come from the state, even if they are affiliated with it, but from the people and the religious formation. In this sense, they determine the norms of society and thus, no project of transformation can be successful unless it is approved by the *'ulama*. In contrast, intellectuals rely on the state and politicized society to support their power.

d. When faced with new circumstances, the *'ulama* have to regenerate, re-evaluate and improve their knowledge and make juristic inferences (*ijtihad*) on contemporary issues. This is true at least for the classical period. On the other hand, intellectuals in Turkey are always

103

conservative; they are unable to generate new ideas, but try to impose previously generated ideas onto society.

The Turkish 'ulama tradition was weakened over time and then vanished at the end of the twentieth century. We can observe three different consequences of the passing of the 'ulama tradition today:

1. Domination by intellectuals, as in Turkey.

2. Domination by sectarian mullahs, as in Iran.

3. Combinations of 'ulama and intellectuals, as seen in Egypt and Pakistan.

Contemporary 'ulama in Turkey have a good knowledge of traditional Islamic jurisprudence (*fiqh*) and Arabic language, but they do not have the ability to use them in actual and current circumstances. So, they only convey information. Since the intellectuals and their technical derivatives, that is, scientists, are nourished by the West, they are also primarily "conveyors." Because both groups lack insight into their nations' cultural and historical realities, they essentially possess the intellectual and scientific heritage that has developed for the realities of other nations. It is difficult to say that intellectuals in the Muslim world have been fully embraced in terms of their profiles, roles, and functions. On the other hand, it is true that while the 'ulama enjoy a highly respected status in public opinion, they are often unable to perform the functions they are assigned.

This situation has resulted in the growth of the new leadership type, which is primarily a profile that merges the intellectual and the 'ulama. A typical example is Fethullah Gülen. While he can analyze a *hadith* meticulously in terms of authenticity, he is simultaneously able to manifest his interpretations on current issues. This new leader type uses the canonical sources of the Qur'an and the Sunna, and has a good knowledge of Islamic sciences and Islamic history, along with contemporary sciences and current developments. In fact, a leader's efficacy diminishes when either of these characteristics is lacking, as in the case of the current Turkish 'ulama, who are cut off from the contemporary world, and Turkish intellectuals, who know nothing about Islam and history.

In essence, the consciousness of Turkish society appears to have been split into two main sections. While one portion takes references from the East and the past, the other takes guidance from the West and the modern. So, Turkey is like a cart with two horses pulling it in opposite directions. Something needs to be done to prevent a devastating split. For that reason, the different segments of society need to engage in dialogue and exert effort to understand each other, and Fethullah Gülen is one of the most important leaders contributing to this effort.

There are two aspects to the dialogue efforts of Fethullah Gülen: the first of these is interfaith dialogue instead of the oft-predicted "clash of civilizations;" the other is dialogue between the two different social segments, state society and civil society. Both dialogue efforts are absolutely vital, and it is important to understand them.

The governing elite in Turkey, as a hard core, is resistant to any development, reform, or legitimate democratic demands. This is one of the reasons for its resisting the ongoing Turkey–European Union negotiations process, despite the fact the same elite has always claimed to be in favor of westernization. Democratic developments and increases in civil initiatives carry the accumulated energy from the periphery towards the center, but resistance at the core continues to cause a waste of social energy.

During the period of the Ottomans, there was a convenient consensus between civil circles and the structure of the state. The structure protected itself with Örfi Law, while civil society and civil initiatives were regulated through Islamic rules and regulations. In other words, Islam protected the individual and the society against the state, political power and the discretionary policies of the rulers.

The state transferred all social functions, except its natural duties, to the society, which performed these duties through its civil institutions and initiatives. This situation not only enabled the state to increase its ability to function in other areas, but it also allowed the state and the society to live together peacefully. With the movement towards westernization, the state changed its policy towards the civil area by increasing its scrutiny, and tried to monitor almost every aspect of social life. One of the main reasons why the elite, which was always in favor of westernization movements, was partly hostile towards Islam was due to the characteristics of injunctions derived from Islamic teachings which protect society from the state. It was thought unless Islam or Islamic law was neutralized, the westernization movement would not be successful. Yet, to perceive modernity and to participate in it is different from associating modernization only with westernization in such a way that it would rule out the religion as a whole.

Therefore, the Turkish history of modernization is a history of tension between people of faith, who would like to have a voice in the civil area, and the state society, which would like to transform the rest of the society in an authoritarian way. The relationship between the state and the religion, the division between the laicist and anti-laicist, and the differentiation between the modernist and conservative, progressive and reactionary, and other such dichotomies, all cause this tension.

Our unfavorable experiences have proved that there is a necessity for dialogue between these two entities. While the present state structure tends to resist all civil society initiatives like those of religious communities, such communities are growing bigger, more widespread, and more influential by using all the means provided by modernization itself, as well as by globalization. Religious communities develop themselves by benefiting from all the facilities and advantages that religion, modernization, and globalization have provided for them.

This tension has emerged because the state has promoted an understanding of secularism as being opposed to religion (that is, laicism) and because the state has always been suspicious of democratic rights, the participation of individuals, civil initiatives, and progress within the society. In this case, it is necessary to build a bridge through dialogue between Civil Islam and the society supported by the state. When we examine in depth Fethullah Gülen's approach to issues such as the state, politics and governance, we realize that he is also opening a door to a dialogue between Civil Islam and state society.

Democracy and the Dialogue between Western and Islamic Legal Cultures: The Gülen Case

Leonid Sykiainen

The significance of any prominent thinker's ideas is determined not only by their intellectual content, their orientation to fundamental sources and convincing quality of argument, but primarily by the role those ideas play at the moment when a society is undergoing a crisis or confronting problems which need to be solved in order to secure its future. Outstanding thinkers can only be described as great if their views affect not only the consciousness and behavior of some limited groups or even nations, but also if they influence the entire system of international relations and the situation in the world in general. Among such thinkers Fethullah Gülen occupies an honorable place.

To explore the depth of Gülen's teaching it is necessary to take into account factors of local, regional and global character. First, it is very important to pay attention to the present situation in the Muslim world, for Gülen is an Islamic thinker anxious about the future of Islamic civilization. Obviously, his ideas belong not only to Muslims, but to the whole world, but Gülen's contribution to global intellectual development is determined by his adherence to Islamic values which can and must serve humankind as a whole.

Here it is necessary to underline that for a long period of time the Muslim World has been experiencing a deep political, social and cultural crisis. On one hand, this crisis directly affects current Islamic thought and education. On the other, it is itself caused by the crisis of Islamic theory and science. This is why Fethullah Gülen's teaching must be evaluated for its

107

impact upon the development of the modern Islamic thought and its contribution to overcoming the crisis of the Muslim World.

Recently, issues of democracy and human rights have again acquired a special importance and are now the most sensitive topic in the dialogue between the West and the Islamic World. These issues are closely linked with another factor which deserves our attention when analyzing Fethullah Gülen's views on democracy: the contemporary stage of the relationships between the West and the Islamic World. All these problems are of special interest and importance when forecasting the development of the Muslim World in the very near future and in particular when evaluating the potential of plans aiming at the promotion of political reforms including democratization in the region of the so-called the Great Middle East, which embraces the majority of Islamic nations.

A consideration of different aspects of the intellectual achievement of Fethullah Gülen is of special interest with respect to the development of democracy in the entire world and the Muslim East especially, as well as maintenance of human rights principles, and the dialogue between different civilizations and cultures, between the West and the East. Currently many western observers make the error of attacking "Islam" when they should be commenting on the approaches or methods of particular activists, that is, they tend to demand reform of "Islam" rather than simply reforming the perspectives of particular people or groups. In the light of this, to explore the views of this outstanding scholar on the key problems of compatibility between Western and Muslim perspectives on democracy and human rights is particularly fruitful

There are different and contradictory views on the issue of democracy. Some Western experts claim Islamic principles and institutions directly contradict democratic values in their modern meaning and for that reason any step made by Muslim societies towards the establishment of democracy must be accompanied by rejecting the Islamic political and legal traditions. Such a position is shared by number of adherents to liberal democratic values both in the West and Russia, and in some Muslim communities. The reverse attitude is adopted by the ideological leaders of Muslim extremists. Claiming that they have the only correct understanding of Islam, they also assert that Islamic fundamentals of power, politics and believers' rights have nothing in common with Western democratic institutions. Even more, those who insist on such extreme understanding of Islamic tradition reject the notion of democracy itself arguing that the power of the people is alien to Islam, which instead of this idea puts forward the principle of the supremacy of Islamic law (Yilmaz 2003:208–237).

Contribution of Islamic Jurisprudence to Legal Culture

It is widely known that Islamic civilization made invaluable contributions to the development of astronomy, mathematics, medicine and navigation. It should also be added that there were a great many prominent Islamic lawyers, whose contribution to world legal thought can hardly be overestimated (Michel 2005).

Law is an important part of the culture of any society. The higher prestige of law and the more active its role in the life of a society, the higher the cultural level of the society. If we consider the place the law occupies in the system of values shared by people as a criterion of the level of the legal culture, then, with good reason, Islamic society can be called a legal one. But Islamic law is not only culture but art, as it embodies both the divine revelation and the art of lawyers (Yilmaz 2005). The human contribution to the development of Islamic jurisprudence has benefited world legal culture and must be acknowledged. In this sense, Islamic law has benefited not only Muslims, but the whole of humanity (Saritoprak 2005).

In fact over many centuries a great variety of views on the fundamentals of the executive and the legislature have developed within Islamic culture, and diverse notions of the relations between the state and the individual have been elaborated. Some of these concepts taken out of the whole context of Islamic thought and addressed to less well-educated Muslims are used to reject the adoption of any democratic idea, or even to justify political extremism (Karliğa 2004:44–62). But within both traditional and modern Islamic political and legal thought, there are several different perspectives on government which are more genuinely representative of the Islamic legal tradition on governing and which do not justify political extremism.

The central place within the theoretical heritage of Islam, as well as in modern Islamic thought, is occupied not by the dogmatic views touched on above, but by quite other values, such as compromise, stability, protection of the life, honor and dignity of the human being, dialogue and consultation.

This position is shared by the most prominent modern Muslim thinkers, jurists, philosophers and politicians. They attract our attention to another feature of Muslim attitudes towards democracy which arises from the fact that Islamic political theory is quite flexible and does not bind Muslims by any rigid limits as far as the choice of concrete forms of government and political system is concerned. The main principle in Islamic political theory is the implementation of three fundamental values: equality, justice and, first of all, consultation. As for their forms and means of enactment, they are vested in the hands of Muslims themselves. Thus, the definite mode of realization of the three pillars can and must take into account the real conditions of Muslims' lives, their traditions, cultural preferences, and other factors.

This position is Gülen's, for he stresses understanding problems of democracy and human rights not in a spirit of formal, dogmatic provisions, but in the light of the fundamental principles and values of Islam, and their sense and meaning, to ensure the maintenance and implementation of major Islamic values, such as justice, equity, and human rights, in our days (Kurtz 2005). Gülen underlines that the modern tendency is to view democracy as a set of political traditions, particular institutions, and cultural assumptions. This notion of democracy runs into problems because the world is a culturally diverse place and no single culture has the monopoly on democratic ideas and practice (Ünal and Williams 2003:147–149).

Gülen believes that Islam understood correctly in an enlightened way and democracy are to a large extent a natural fit. They are both mobile and flexible ideas which are easily adapted in different societies and carry universal values with similar basic elements. Both Islam and democracy hold that all human beings are equal and each person in addition to his rights has certain responsibilities to society. At its core each of the two treats human beings with respect and asks them to treat others the same way.

Interaction between Islamic and European Legal Cultures

Islamic law is one of the main legal systems of the modern world. It has a number of features that distinguish it from other legal cultures. At the same time, its common principles and the majority of its concrete norms are similar to fundamental ideas and particular provisions of other legal systems. It has always been a characteristic of *shari'a* to cooperate closely with other legal cultures. The foregoing development of the Muslim legal world laid the ground for the interest in European legal models in many Muslim countries in the 19th century, and accounts for the fact that Islamic law, on the one hand, was receptive to foreign experience, and on the other hand, was able to enrich other legal cultures. Islamic and European legal cultures now interact even more intensively in the modern legal systems of Muslim countries. This interaction accounts for the main features of the law which is practiced in many Muslim countries today.

Gülen points out some differences between Western and Islamic notions of good government. Namely, for Islam the most significant aspect of good government lies not in the existence of formal institutions such as elections, parliamentary institutions, or political parties, and even not in providing particular rights, but in its contents which must be aimed at protecting concrete Islamic values—security of belief, life, mind, dignity, and property—though the above mentioned institutions themselves are essential as an important means for securing these values and goals.

Gülen stresses that the Islamic understanding of democracy is based mainly on the concept of *shura* (collective and community consultation). For him, consultation is an essential foundation of the Muslim community (Gülen 2005b:43–58). It is a method, a process of government and way of life for Muslims. In the political field, shura in general corresponds to modern democracy.

It must be pointed out that the Qur'anic verses ordering the believers to seek, follow and apply collective consultation are without any qualifications or limitations (Qur'an 42:38). Thus, all members of an Islamic state are eligible for giving or requesting consultation, which can be sought or requested with regard to any matter, except a matter covered by a clear-cut revelation from God. Consequently, all political matters such as those concerning the selection of the ruler, the structure and shape of the government, the form of political system, the running of the government and of the various affairs of the state, and all other related matters are to be decided by consultation through the participation of all the eligible members of the community.

So, in public and government affairs collective consultation is concerned with two main issues: the selection of the head of state and running of the government together with reviewing the legality and propriety of governmental and presidential actions. With regard to the first issue, the selection of the head of the state, Gülen underlines that collective consultation is very flexible and adopts various forms. Elections, whether direct or indirect, are considered by Gülen to be an Islamic method of selecting the head of state or members of the legislative body which satisfies the consultation process.

With regard to the second issue, the running of the government and control over the legality and propriety of the executive's actions, Islamic law is also very flexible. The establishment of a representative body through direct or indirect elections is compatible with Islam and is a good application of community and collective consultation. In addition to their reviewing authorities, representative bodies may be empowered to legislate on different matters provided that such regulations do not violate any unambiguous and clear-cut principle or rule of Islamic injunctions. Gülen's view is that Muslims may live in any country or community which respects human rights, equity and justice.

According to Gülen's approach, the establishment of political parties is also compatible with Islamic law, and they can operate freely within an Islamic state if they satisfy two conditions: they must recognize Islam as a religion and law and must not act against Islam nor work for or serve the enemies of the Muslim nations.

In other words, according to Gülen's teaching, in the political field and matters of government, *shura* within Islam corresponds to democracy in Western systems. If democracy is the government of the people by the people for the people, shura is a process which guarantees that all affairs of the people are decided by the people and for their interests. So, the basics of democracy and the fundamentals of shura in the political field are alike; these two notions are not opposed.

This position differs somewhat from the traditional Islamic concept of collective consultation which was more responsibility-oriented than rights-oriented. But this genuine Islamic idea can be interpreted as one of the most basic human rights and a means of protecting and preserving all other human rights under Islamic law, especially the right to equality, the freedom of thought, and the right to express oneself freely in order to correct or demand the correction of what is not right. Everyone has the right and even bears the obligation to correct or demand correction of injustices and other wrongful acts, even if committed by the highest governmental officials, including the ruler himself. As such, consultation in this interpretation becomes the most indispensable guarantee for all human rights in Islam.

In addition to the modern understanding of Islamic collective consultation Gülen pays special attention to the political process and methods of ensuring political goals. He does not believe in using religion as a political device as mixing politics and religion always degrades religion. He is also categorically opposed to the use of violence to attain political ends. Gülen stresses the importance of law and order in society and does not believe that respect for others can be instilled by force or that a modern world can be built by repression. Far from it, he insists that in today's world the most effective way to demonstrate the validity of any value is through persuasion and rational reasoning. Thus, he describes those who resort to force as intellectually bankrupt (Gülen 2005b:59–66).

The thinker insists that very single right is respected in Islam and cannot be violated. In particular, the right of an individual cannot be violated for the interest of the community (Gülen 2004a:1–4). This idea is central to Gülen's approach to the concept of human rights in Islam and the interpretation of Islamic tradition with regard to this issue. He recalls that if there are nine criminals and only one innocent person on a ship, in order to punish the criminals, Islam does not permit the sinking of that ship because of the innocent person. The Qur'an, Gülen continues, declares that one who takes a life unjustly is as if he took the lives of the whole of humankind. Also, Prophet Muhammad said that the Muslim was one who did no harm to others with either his tongue or hand.

Gülen demonstrates that Islamic perspectives do not conflict with human rights principles. These very principles must be the starting point in the modern interpretation of the Islamic tradition. It is significant that, just as in the western liberal view, Gülen takes group rights to be conditional on individual ones. Following this principle Gülen proposes that the Qur'an and the obligation of Muslims to obey the word of God assist us in the development of Islamic notions of human rights. For example, the rights of the individual and the freedom of worship are reflected verses such as "There is no compulsion in religion."

Gülen analyzes the different rights recognized in Islam, including freedom of religion and belief, thought and expression, to own property and the sanctity of one's home, to marry and have children, to communicate and to travel, and the right to an unimpeded education (Ünal and Williams 2000:135-138). He underlines that the principles of Islamic jurisprudence are based on these and other rights, all of which have now been accepted by modern legal systems, such as the protection of life, religion, property, family life, and intellect, as well as the basic understanding of the equality of people, which is based on the fact that all people are human beings, and subsequently, the rejection of all racial, color, and linguistic discrimination. Gülen draws our attention to the fact that all these values have been protected as separate principles in modern legal systems which consider them indispensable.

Gülen's approach to the problem of human rights confirms that he is one of the most prominent thinkers and contributes a great deal to the elaboration of modern Islamic concepts of human rights compared with Western liberal theory. Democracy, Gülen argues, though it still needs to be further improved, is now the only viable political form, and people should seek to modernize and consolidate democratic institutions in order to build a society where individual rights and freedom are respected and protected. But, stressing his personal adherence to Islam, Gülen underlines that people everywhere always demand freedom of choice within their beliefs, that is, in the way they run their affairs and in their expression of spiritual and religious values.

How can Muslims' aspirations be turned into reality, not by throwing Islamic traditions away, but within them? Gülen's answer is quite clear. He rejects the notion that Islam is dogmatic and stresses the separation of the eternal and the evolving judgments of Islamic jurisprudence. Specifically, political affairs in general and democratic institutions and human right in particular are covered by Islamic legislative provisions which can and must change from place to place, from era to era, and along with evolving circumstances.

Gülen points out that democracy has developed and evolved over time. Just as it has gone through many stages in the past, it will continue to evolve to refine itself in the future. Islamic principles of equality, tolerance, and justice can help in this regard provided that the injunctions of the Qur'an and the Sunna as well as any definite *shari'a* judgments are re-examined, rebuilt and restored in the light of advancing knowledge and changes in societies.

For the sake of this re-examination Fethullah Gülen emphasizes that one of the factors facilitating the Islamic interpretation of democracy is the belief that Muslims can and must interpret the divine law. Gülen also draws our attention to the fact that *ijtihad* (Gülen 2004b:xix) itself provides for different nations to learn from one another, and hence he does not reject the use of any Western forms of democracy. Rather, he advises giving such adopted institutions an Islamic dimension and in this way reconciling secularist and religious political theories. Gülen believes that Islamic government shares many joint aspects with its ideological counterparts, yet it has its own unique vision with regard to political methodology.

So, Gülen's approach is powerful proof of the democratic ideas propagated by Islam as he is convinced that Islamic democracy and secular political liberalization are not two separate phenomena. In other words, Gülen is contributing to the theory of Islamic law specifically as far as notions of *ijtihad* and "exclusive interests" *(masail mursala)* are concerned. (Yilmaz 2003:203–237)

Role of Islamic Legal Culture for Dialogue between Civilizations

Gülen points out that the dominant Islamic culture in the Muslim World coexists with democratic arrangements on the global level. So, the concept of modernization and democratization does not inevitably mean Westernization but can involve the possibility of adoption of many Western democratic achievements within the Islamic framework.

The value of Muslim legal culture is not limited to exclusively legal questions. It can and must play an important positive role in addressing more general, even global issues. In particular, the legal achievements of Islamic law can help to launch a constructive dialogue between the Islamic world and the West, their cooperation in solving such complex issues as globalization, human rights, and even the struggle with extremism and international terrorism. The language of law

is universal in the present-day world and modern Muslim legal thought should
play a more active role in the development of contemporary civilization. Islamic jurisprudence is a great art and an important component of Islamic civilization. It is currently rather neglected but should be studied to a much greater extent by Muslim and non-Muslim legal scholars alike.

Taking into account these ideas, Gülen defends Islam in its civilized, enlightened understanding emphasizing the compatibility between Islam, knowledge, and science. He believes that the reality of the contemporary world is too complex for the understanding of any single person and thus that experts from different fields, such as the particular areas of science, ethics, religion, and so forth should all be consulted and cooperate about important issues. He stresses that issues that concern all communities should not be dealt with in a sectarian way; the consultation process should be open to other points of view on religious teaching. He has therefore done much to promote a dialogue between communities. Gülen is convinced that dialogue, education and tolerance are the only way for forward for the world in our times. He reminds us that issues relating to an individual or the actions of an individual should not affect our attitudes towards a group of people. He also does not accept political domination by a religious clergy; he is sure that secularist and religious values and ideas can live peacefully side by side in the same society. This last idea is very important in context of the Turkey–European Union dialogue.

By his thoughts Fethullah Gülen proves that he is an outstanding contributor to Islamic thought. It is known that traditional Islamic thought distinguishes three main fundamentals of power and politics: consultation, equality and justice. Gülen adds to them new ones: tolerance, dialogue, positive activism, education, and cooperation against common enemies and concerns. These pillars are not of lesser importance than the first three, as they reflect specific features of our world as well as the relationship of Islam with the other cultures and faiths (Gülen 2004a:37–45).

The main principle of Gülen's teachings is an intellectual and spiritual enlightenment drawn from the traditional sources of Islam. His methodology is bottom-up and individual-centered. He advises Muslims to educate themselves and use the resources within Islamic intellectual tradition and culture to contribute to the contemporary world. In his call for dialogue and tolerance Gülen remains adherent to Islamic civilization. His intellectual activity shows that Muslims can develop and establish the future through an intellectual and spiritual revival which reflects the world's realities. By his achievements, Gülen proves that Islamic intellectual heritage and political culture must be revisited and respected and that Muslims' progress depends on the development of Islamic sciences and education. As for Islamic political culture and democracy, they will become powerful not by their isolation from or opposition to others but by giving of their own achievements and taking the best from others.

The Juxtaposition of Islam and Violence

Ismail Albayrak

This essay considers the use of violence for political ends from an Islamic perspective. We examine what core Islamic texts say about violence and terror; the relationship between the notion of *jihad* and Islam; the status of suicide attacks in Islam; and the false justification of war in the modern world, which paves the way for terrorist actions. We address these issues through the perspectives of the eminent Turkish scholar and thinker Fethullah Gülen. The paper concludes with a summary of the effects of interfaith and intercultural dialogue meetings initiated by Gülen both within and outside Turkey in order to promote national and international tolerance, peace, and mutual understanding.

Terrorism is perpetrated across borders, causes global unrest, and creates anarchy, fear and uncertainty. Its cruel and ruthless disregard of laws and ethics was shown in the attacks of 9/11. In addition, now that terrorists potentially have access to chemical, nuclear and biological weapons, the possibility of mass destruction has increased significantly. Everybody feels vulnerable to a terrorist attack and many live in a continual state of fear. The terrorists who have unleashed this global calamity, however, do not see themselves as guilty. Furthermore, their attacks and the responses to them only serve to increase their internal solidarity, resistance, unity and conviction of their own righteousness. Consequently, these organized activities produce a polarity between "us" and "them." We observe sadly that some media members, scholars, politicians, strategists and other institutions, contributing to this polarization, easily associate our common problem, namely terrorism, with Islam and Muslims, and thus Muslims are quickly categorized as "them." The approach of Gülen to this complex problem is extremely important due

119

to the difficulty of formulating and sustaining a balanced view. Gülen's approach to terror eschews easy emotionalism and prejudice and seeks to embrace all humanity. Before examining Gülen's approach to the status of terror in Islam, we will consider the relationship between war and the notion of *jihad*.

It should first be emphasized that one of the greatest sins in Islam is killing a person. Allah says in Sura Nisa (Qur'an 4:93) "If a man kills a believer intentionally, his reward is Hell for ever. Allah's wrath is against him and He has cursed him and prepared for him an awful doom." The eminent companion exegete Abd Allah ibn Abbas interprets this verse to mean that the repentance of those who kill a believer purposefully will be denied, and they will be doomed to eternal Hell (al-Tabari 1954: vol. 4, 295; Çapan 2004:82). Interestingly, when we look at the main source of Islam, namely the Qur'an, it will be seen that killing innocent people is mentioned together with associating other gods with Allah (Qur'an 27:68). Also, while killing a person is considered one of the most grievous sins, Islam also strictly prohibits suicide. According to Islamic law, one has no right to end one's own life or damage one's body; the argument that one owns one's life or body is erroneous. The reason for this lies in the Qur'an: "Verily We have honored the children of Adam. We carry them on the land and the sea, and have made provision of good things for them, and have preferred them above many of those whom We created with a marked preferment" (Qur'an 17:70). (Please also find the hadith relating to what the Prophet said about suicide being haram and leading to eternal punishment etc.) The Qur'an thus gives honor and glory to all mankind equally, and considers killing one innocent person (including oneself) equal to killing the whole of humankind (Qur'an 5:32). This point is crucially important because it demonstrates that Islam considers killing to be a crime against not only Muslims but all humanity. Moreover, the Qur'an places great emphasis on the virtue of peace (Qur'an 4:128), and does not permit anyone to respond to an evil deed with one which is worse; instead, it says "Repel the evil deed with one which is better" (Qur'an 41:34). Sound reason also suggests this teaching. Injustice should not be resisted by sowing the seeds of revulsion and hatred among people.

Another important Islamic concept is *jihad*. This term is often simplified by mistakenly associating it only with war and offering shallow arguments concerning its meaning. This reductionist approach to the term narrows the comprehensiveness of the notion of *jihad*. This key Qur'anic term is one of Islam's most important concepts which embraces both the material and the spiritual life of mankind.

Jihad does not mean simply a holy war. Although the word *jihad* and its conjugations are repeated some thirty-four times in the Qur'an, only four of these usages (Qur'an 9:41, 73; 25:52; 66:9) refer directly to war (Karlığa 2004:39). *Jihad*, as Gülen has stated in general terms, is every kind of effort made by believers to obtain God's approval and to satisfy Him. There are various dimensions of *jihad* (strife, fighting, and endeavor). It is possible to categorize them as physical, psychological, sociological, and intellectual jihads. For instance, God equates those who work for widows and the poor with those who make *jihad* for God (al-Bukhari 1981:Nafaqa, 1; Al-Hajjaj 1982:Zuhd, 41; Karlığa 2004:40). In another place the Prophet informs us that the greatest *jihad* is a *jihad* made against one's self (al-Tirmidhi: Fadail al-Jihad, 2). As Gülen explains: *Jihad* is purification and seeking perfection to please God; cleansing the mind, by means of Qur'anic verses, from false preconceptions, thoughts, and superstitions; expelling impurities from the heart through prayer; asking for forgiveness; austerity (*riyada*); and studying the Qur'an, Hadith, and other knowledge with a purified heart and mind.[1] Interestingly, the Prophet's description of war as a minor *jihad* shows clearly the object of the major *jihad*: in Islamic understanding *jihad* means an individual's struggle against Satan. Briefly, *jihad* is a form of worship which embraces the material and spiritual dimensions of mankind. War is limited to the external or physical aspect of this struggle and constitutes only a small part of jihad. Islam fixes the boundaries of both major and minor *jihads* and it should be remembered that these boundaries and dimensions are not only legal but also humane and ethical.

Considering the life of humankind most honorable and issuing many rules for the preservation of human happiness in this world and the hereafter, Islam acts with proper prudence to stop war, terror, injustice, and anarchy. Nevertheless, we know that Islam allows Muslims to fight in particular situations, which it regards as *arizi* (unnatural) and secondary. Peace, however, is essential in Islam. War is justified only to prevent chaos (which leads to wars), anarchy, tyranny, mischief, rebellion and so on. The Qur'an explains this issue (Qur'an 2:191) by stating "tumult and oppression are worse than slaughter." Thus war is justified in these exceptional

---

[1] Fethullah Gülen, in an interview with the Italian Journalist Michele Zanzucchi

circumstances. Islamic law acknowledges that Muslims have the right to protect their religion, life, property, progeny, and their honor and sacred values. But Islam was the first religion in human history to codify regulations of war on the basis of rights and justice. In Sura Mâida, Allah says "O those who believe! Stand out firmly for God as witnesses to fair dealing and let not the hatred of others to you make you swerve to wrong and depart from justice. Be just; that is next to piety; and fear God for God is well acquainted with all that you do." Islam allows war only to prevent anarchy; it does not sanctify war undertaken in order to compel people of other religions to convert to Islam or to bring the whole world under Islamic sovereignty (*Dar al-Islam*). In other words, Islam contains no concept of "holy war" in this issue. If a Muslim country is secure, war is not obligatory. In addition, it is not legitimate to declare war against any people only on the basis of their disbelief (*kufr*). There is also no claim in Islam to make the entire world Muslim. The Qur'an states clearly "Not all people will believe" (Bulaç 2004:56).

We should now examine the Islamic principles concerning the conduct of war. First of all Islam states clearly that individuals may not start a war on behalf of Muslims. A person cannot issue a *fatwa* (legal pronouncement) to fight against another country, nation, group or individuals. The reason for this is quite simple: according to Islamic law, the declaration or initiation of a war is the duty of a state in accordance with certain principles. When the state initiates a war it must obey certain principles. According to Gülen, in war Islam defines the limits that constrain the treatment of the enemy. We see the best example of this at a time near the death of the Prophet. When he was ill, news came that the Northern Arabs, along with the Byzantines, were preparing an attack on Medina. The Prophet ordered the preparation of an army under the command of Uthama bin Zayd, and gave the following instructions to Uthama: "Fight in God's way. Do not be cruel to people. Do not go against your covenant. Do not cut down trees bearing fruits. Do not slaughter livestock. Do not kill the pious who are secluded in monasteries, engaged in worship, or children and women" (Aktan 2004:26). The instructions of the Prophet were enshrined in Islamic legal literature, to the effect that the killing of non-combatants such as women, children, the elderly, the disabled is expressly forbidden (Tahawi 1996: vol. 3, 224; Çapan 2004:83). There is no Islamic text which allows the killing of civilians in war, because they are held to be not combatant (*muharib*).

The Qur'an states clearly "Fight in God's way (in order to exalt His name) against those who fight against you, but do not transgress the bounds (set by God), for surely God loves not those who transgress the bounds" (Qur'an 2:190). The Arabic verb *yuqâtilûna* in the verse is of extreme importance. To explain this in grammatical terms, the mood (reciprocal form) in Arabic denotes "participation" which, in this sense, means "those who fall under the status of combatant." Thus, non-combatants are not to be fought against. This rule must be obeyed in war and applies equally stringently when war has not been declared. In addition to this, according to Islamic law, Muslims may not start a war without informing their enemy, and if the enemy calls on them to negotiate a settlement the Muslim forces must cease fighting.

Thus, when the war starts Muslim fighters should not kill civilians; indeed, the Qur'an (Qur'an 2:190) warns Muslims not to transgress the limits of war even against the soldiers of the enemy. "Transgression" means killing civilians, torturing the enemy's soldiers, not respecting the dead bodies of the enemy, not meeting the basic needs of enemy prisoners, and not obeying the rules of war. It is important to note that Islam prohibits transgression in the form of reprisal. For example, if the enemy's soldiers rape Muslim women, Muslim soldiers should not rape the women of the enemy's community. This prohibition also applies to the torture of captured soldiers, to attacks on civilians, and so on. It is known that when the Muslims in Andalusia (Spain) were expelled from the peninsula, some Muslims asked the Ottoman Sultan Mehmed II to expel his Christian subjects from Istanbul as retaliation for the Christians' attacks on the Andalusian Muslims. However, the Ottoman Shaikh al-Islam Zambilli Jamali Efendi objected, arguing that this practice was against Islamic law concerning the rights of non-Muslim subjects (Karlığa 1998:16). In brief, Islam forbids reprisal and the frame of every action in war is defined by Islamic law, which nobody may transgress.

As shown above, Islam insists on the legal rights of the enemy soldier in war, even though it is difficult to maintain a balance in a combat situation. If the enemy is protected by Islam, the civilian is protected even more stringently. No one may hurt an innocent person; no one may be a suicide bomber rushing into crowds with bombs tied to his or her body; no one may kidnap innocent civilians and behead them, no matter what their religion. Moreover, as it bans attacking civilians in war, Islam considers attacking civilians in peace as the most grievous sin. The Qur'an, as has been mentioned above, equates killing innocent people with unbelief (25:68; 6:151).

The individuality of a crime is basic principle in Islam; whoever commits a crime is the only person to be called to account. As repeatedly stated in the Qur'an "no bearer of a burden can bear the burden of another" (Qur'an 6:164; 16:15; 35:18). Therefore, it is not permissible in Islam to issue a fatwa allowing a crime against civilians to be carried out. It is obvious that such attacks are indiscriminate except in the sense that civilians rather than military personnel are deliberately targeted. Such indiscriminate attacks are totally incompatible with one of the general principles of Islamic law (Çapan 2004:89). The proposition that any action is legitimate in order to achieve an undefined goal is contrary to Islam. The example used by Gülen is as follows: if there are nine guilty persons and one innocent on a ship, this ship should not be sunk; the innocent should not be sacrificed to punish the guilty majority (Gülen 2003a:200).

Thus, those who attack the lives of innocent people in the name of religion will lose their happiness in this world and salvation in the hereafter. Islam is a true faith and it should be lived truly. As Gülen has pointed out, faith cannot be attained by the use of untrue methods. In Islam, just as a goal must be legitimate, so must all the means employed to reach that goal. From this perspective it is clear that one cannot achieve Heaven by murdering another person.[2] Considering that human life is the most precious thing in Islam, the gravity of the present situation is obvious. Gülen, who publicly condemned the actions of the terrorists behind the attack of 9/11, calls upon everybody to condemn those who are darkening the bright face of Islam, and to take collective action against them. As an Islamic scholar and an expert in this field, Gülen finds it unacceptable to associate Islam with terrorism. He declares that a Muslim must not be a terrorist and a terrorist cannot be a true Muslim (Hermann 2004).[3]

As we stated above, individual cannot declare war; only the state can do so. Today, those who carry out suicide attacks are acting contrary to the principles of their religion, and perpetrating irreligious acts in the name of

---

[2] Fethullah Gülen, in an interview with the Italian journalist Michele Zanzucchi; in "Dünyada Zihni Kirlilik," *Aksiyon*, October 12, 2004.

[3] Rainer Hermann (2004), "Fethullah Gülen Offers Antidote For Terror," *Frankfurter Allgemeine* April 13, 2004

religion. Gülen insists that Islamic principles should be tested by the consensus of Muslim scholars. This shows his reliance on and trust in Islamic sources and the tradition which has carried these sources and their interpretation from age to age up until today. Thus, a few unqualified extremists' fatwas approving suicide attacks which are not confirmed by the Muslim community do not represent the view taken by Islam and its true followers. Neither is it reasonable, therefore, to attribute a terrorist act to the religion of a particular terrorist. The terrorist might be Muslim, Christian or Jewish but this does not mean that his or her act is an Islamic, a Christian, or a Jewish act. So, the phrase "Islamic terror" is regarded as an insult to pious, sincere and innocent Muslims all over the world; a few uneducated, discontented, misled fanatics should not be taken to represent countless sincere believers.

From the Qur'anic perspective, attention should be paid to the relationship between the concept of *sulh* (peace) and the concept of *sâlih amal* (good deeds). *Sâlih*, like *sulh*, comes from the same root and means "to cleave to peace or move towards peace." Gülen holds that this peace is a result of *tawhid* (Unity of God/Oneness of God) and that Islam, being a religion of Unity, ensures universal unity, equality, peace and cooperation among humankind (Aydüz 2004:227). Briefly, Islam is a religion of peace and safety and "Muslim" means a trustworthy, peaceful and reliable person. The Prophet Muhammad described the Muslim as a person from whose hand and tongue people are safe.

Having summarized the status of suicide attacks in Islam, we will focus on the causes of these activities, their historical background and some solutions in the light of Gülen's views. At the beginning of this paper we noted that Gülen approaches the problem from various angles, considering religious, political, social, psychological and economic dimensions. At this juncture we place great stress on his critical re-evaluation of the approaches to terrorist activities adopted by both Muslims and non-Muslims. Gülen states that both Muslims and non-Muslims are responsible for the instability of the world today.

Concerning Muslims, he argues that some thoughtless people who lack the power of discernment narrow the broad scope of Islam. For this reason Gülen suggests that such people must first change the image of Islam in their mind. Because they have no comprehensive understanding of the sources, they take as their reference only some sections of the Islamic sources without exploring the Qur'an and the Prophetic tradition, or the understandings of prominent Muslim scholars. They read these texts literally and mostly out of context without examining what precedes or follows them. The results are disastrous: they misinterpret their religion and then put this misunderstanding into practice; consequently they are misguided and they misguide others. Muslims should, Gülen says, begin to re-evaluate the fatwas of the people who say they represent Islam today, because today everybody experiences directly or indirectly the damage of the terror which arises from this intolerance and misinterpretation. Furthermore, Gülen emphasizes the danger of the idea of carrying out terrorist acts under the pretence of "representing the oppressed nations of the world" against the people of other nations; this notion is by no means compatible with Islam. Terror does harm to Islam, Muslims, and humanity at large. In fact, Gülen thinks that an Islamic world does not really exist today, as Muslims are divided and scattered throughout the world. Today Muslims are not able to communicate with one another and constitute a union, or to work together to solve common problems. Thus, he believes that at the moment Muslims often do not contribute to the world peace effectively (Gülen 2004a:2–3).

There are a number of ossified problems in the Muslim world, and the existence of these problems makes it easy for some evil powers to manipulate the vulnerable. Moreover, the ongoing problems of poverty, lack of education for the poor, states' inability to unite with their citizens, a deficient understanding of the notion of the social state, a lack of democratic governments which give priority to the rights and freedoms of their citizens, and, most importantly, the neglect of the spiritual and ethical life of the people have led to a deterioration of the general condition of the Muslim world (Gülen 2003a:202). All these explanations show clearly that war waged against terrorist organizations by police or military forces will not be sufficient to stop them. Gülen has stated that to fight against the ideology of the terrorists we need the arguments of intellectuals. Gülen also notes that one cannot establish order on the basis of rude power; military measures can only result in disorder and injustice (Gülen 200a3:202). It is also generally acknowledged that an order achieved by mere force and rude power cannot last long. Gülen expresses his dissatisfaction with the explanation that the reason behind these terrorist activities is religion and points out that when religion is held to be the source of violence, the major factor and power goes unnoticed (Gülen 2003a:202).

We will consider now Gülen's approach to the problem of overcoming this global calamity of terror. It is important to note that, in contrast to many observers, Gülen, while acknowledging certain negative developments, thinks that the world situation is not deteriorating and there will be no clash of civilizations. According to Gülen, those who are looking forward to a catastrophic future for the world and a clash of civilizations are individuals or groups who are unable to impose their world view on the people and hope that global antagonisms will ensure the continuation of their power in the world (Aydüz 2004:237). Nonetheless, the global political situation does not look very hopeful, and we should not be complacent. Gülen emphasizes that education must play a very important role in helping to resolve the world's problems; his experience has thought him that the key problem of our modern civilization is the education of mankind (Ergene 2004:47). Today, many schools and other educational centers established on his advice and initiative both within Turkey and outside Turkey are making very good progress to achieve this aim.

Besides education, another important activity initiated by Gülen in the cause of world peace is dialogue meetings. As Ergene has pointed out, these meetings are an extension of Gülen's global educational activities; they also serve the education of humanity. Although he has been severely criticized by some people, he bravely argues that these dialogue meetings are primarily concerned with religion and are thus a religious duty.[4] Gülen insists on the religious nature of the meetings because the basic Islamic sources advise Muslims to engage in dialogue with other faiths. Thus, Gülen says that dialogue is not his invention or innovation but a revival of the most neglected aspect of Islam. His constancy in this regard is very sincere: he has said that even if the sensitive political balance of the world changes a thousand times he will never stop the dialogue meetings because the Islamic sources do not allow him to stop them.[5] For Gülen, dialogue and tolerance mean accepting every person irrespective of their status and learning to live together.[6] He is concerned to show that the rights of religion, life, travel, trade, property, free

---

[4] www.herkul.org
[5] www.herkul.org
[6] www.herkul.org

speech, and so on are guaranteed by the Prophetic tradition, the best examples being the document of Medina and the farewell speech of the Prophet Muhammad. Although there are ten years between these two events, Gülen says, there is no difference between them in their approaches to the rights of non-Muslims (Jews, Christians) and even of unbelievers. For Gülen this indicates clearly the religious imperative to continue the dialogues. Gülen also accepts that due to a lack of dialogue, some mistakes have been made by Muslims in the history of Islam, but he argues that the history of Islam is also full of good examples of dialogue. It is very important to note here that Gülen makes reference to the synthesis of Turkish mysticism and Islam. Anatolian mystics developed their understanding of love on the basis of the motto "Because we love the Creator we love all His creatures" (Ergene 2004:17). This point is surely crucial for the understanding of Gülen's dialogue activities for world peace.

Thus, the key word in Gülen's dialogue meetings is love, and this love derives from his understanding of Islam and Sufism practiced in Anatolia. Those who seek to profit from chaos, violence and terror will doubtless fail to understand the conception of love in Gülen's philosophy and will consequently fail to understand Gülen's world view. Philosophically speaking, Gülen, like his predecessor Said Nursi, considers love to be the essence of creation: according to Gülen, love is the most essential element, the brightest light, the greatest power in every creature in the world. If one is grounded in love, every kind of difficulty in the world can be overcome (Gülen 2003a:17). Thus, Gülen introduces love as an unquestionable condition for being human. Without love, it is almost impossible to create an atmosphere conducive to dialogue and tolerance. Gülen's love is not an empty conceptualization; it is directly related to his religion, whose commandments he sensitively tries to put into practice. Gülen says that religion commands love and peace; love makes people truly human and the spirits of the true will rise to Heaven (Gülen 2003a:17). Clearly, then, love lights the fuse of dialogue and global tolerance; it paves the way to global peace. For Gülen, man can only communicate actively with all humans and other creatures through love, which leads him to help others (Gülen 2003a:47). Unlike ideologies based on social Darwinism, which suggest that only the powerful are fit to live and the weak should not survive, Gülen, as a Muslim scholar, holds that love derived from Islam has a great capacity to embrace every person in the world irrespective of their beliefs. Relying on his own conviction and tradition, and on the global transmitters of love such as Abu Hanifa, Ahmad Yasawi, Mawlana Jalal al-Din al-Rumi, Imam Ghazali, and Imam Rabbani, Gülen describes love and tolerance as "the roses and flowers of our hill" (Gülen 2003a:78). But this love must be expressed in its practical and living dimension, and so Gülen has organized many meetings, in which different people with different religious and cultural backgrounds come together to discuss the common problems of humanity. The participants in these meetings have initiated various projects and offered many solutions to ameliorate the chaotic situation in our world. Most importantly, these meetings show the people that dialogue is the real remedy for terror, chaos, and intolerance. Gülen, as a sincere believer in the importance of dialogue, has asked his close friends not to name this unfinished process of dialogue to emphasize that this process is a long way from completion. This also shows his optimistic view of the future.

We have tried to show that Islam and terror are radically opposed concepts, even though some manipulative, uneducated, or deceived individuals commit terrorist crimes in the name of religion. We have also drawn attention to the mistaken association of *jihad* with war. We then pointed out that Islam considers killing innocent people in the name of religion to be the greatest sin, and has never legitimized suicide. Next, we focused on Gülen's emphasis on the importance of dialogue. Love is situated in the heart of his understanding of dialogue, and this love is nurtured by his faith in Islam and his mystical understanding of religion. Ali, the cousin of the Prophet, declared that he saw Muslims as his religious fellows and non-Muslims as his fellows in creation. Gülen agrees. This love necessitates dialogue not only with human beings but also with all creatures. When humankind realizes this dialogue, God's consent will be achieved. This is, according to Gülen, the purpose of man's existence in the world.

Leaving Footprints in Houston:
Answers to Questions on Women and the Gülen Movement

Anna J. Stephenson

Feminists are questioning whether M. Fethullah Gülen, the Gülen movement, and individuals inspired by the movement promote advancement of women's status in family and public life by enabling women to hold power in public positions and have an equal role with men in developing social and religious worldviews, or whether they perpetuate limits on women in professional leadership roles and dissuade them from challenging status quo gender beliefs (Göle 2003; Turam 2000; White 2002). This concern is part of a broader examination of the extent to which the Turkish state's top-down modernizing reforms over the past hundred years as well as Muslim intellectuals' efforts to apply Turkish-Muslim activism Islamism in contemporary society have increased women's status, self-determination, and equal opportunity in a culture characterized by patriarchal gender norms (Arat 1996; Arat 1997; Arat 1998; Kagitcibasi 1986; Kandiyoti 1998). Women's contributions to society through family life, volunteerism, and lower paying professions should never be discounted. However, feminists focus on equal opportunity in public professions and thought leadership on the premise that these are essential for women to gain and maintain status in both public society and family life (Kagitcibasi 1986). Also, as the Gülen movement is increasingly important in "defining the contemporary global Islamic experience" (Voll 2003: 238), it has a duty to exemplify women's equal opportunity at all levels to use their talents for economic security, professional achievement, and thought leadership in developing an Islamic worldview.

131

Feminists analyze the Gülen movement as a whole as well as the lives of individual women living in Turkey and in the movement's philanthropic communities in developing countries. They find the status and roles of these middle- and upper-class moderate Turkish Islamists (those seeking to influence society through social versus political means) reflect freedoms as well as limits on women that have developed in the Turkish state's and moderate Islamism's modernizing efforts (Turam 2000; White 2002; Yavuz 2003b). Turam (2000) offers two major critiques. First, Mr. Gülen's ideas encourage women to hold professional or volunteer positions outside their homes in accord with legal reforms. However, his thoughts on gender roles can also lead to limits found in wider Turkish culture on women's professional and leadership equality with men. Second, women inspired by Gülen's understanding of Islam are widely complicit with these limiting gender norms.

This essay adds to the discussion of these two critiques by offering my qualitative research into and interpretations of life histories from Turkish women inspired by Mr. Gülen who were living in Houston, Texas, during 2004 (Stephenson 2005). Interpreting life histories brings to light examples of women's perspectives on social issues as demonstrated in their everyday practices and major life decisions (Abu-Lughod 1993; Allport 1965; Coles 2001; Vandsemb 1995). I interpreted life histories in the framework of practice theory, which views cultures, norms, and worldviews from the perspective of being experienced and lived out in everyday practices by individuals acting for their own benefit (Bourdieu 1977; de Certeau 1984; Ortner 1996). Practice theory is especially relevant today when the speed at which a myriad of possible beliefs and life ways are shared around the globe expands the possible life choices for many people (Appadurai 1996; Ong 1999). Individuals' consciousness of influencing culture from "bottom-up" is still being questioned, as is their actual power to improve their life chances (Lamphere et al. 1997; Ong 1999; Ortner 1996).

One of Mr. Gülen's most influential ideas is that individuals contribute by their everyday lives to social discourses on Turkish identity, faith, and remedies for social problems. They can model disciplined and moral lives, be financially and intellectually successful, give time and money to support development projects nationwide and worldwide, and raise an ethical and well-rounded generation that can be part of national and international leadership (Gülen 2004b; Ünal and Williams 2000; Yavuz 2003).

The movement's emphasis on media and transnationalism (Ong 1999; Schiller, Basch, and Blanc 1994) also promotes global sharing of worldviews and possible life choices (Yavuz and Esposito 2003). As life histories from participants in the Gülen movement living in Houston demonstrate, women in the movement practice this informal process of creating social change through everyday life to make a place for themselves in public society as Muslims and to influence limiting gender norms. Women who do not formally resist limitations may do so informally both verbally and in their life choices (Abu-Lughod 1998; Lamphere et al. 1997; Ortner 1996).

In the context of socially acceptable life possibilities available to Turkish women inspired by Gülen, what do the following examples of choices and concerns say about their views on gender norms in the Gülen movement and Turkish culture? Is achieving leadership roles in formal religious interpretation and the movement's public activities important to them at this time? What limitations are important to them now? In what ways do they negotiate, legitimize, question, and even resist limitations? Although this qualitative research into individual lives does not account for everything about women in the movement, it does present some ways women think about and negotiate gender norms.

Gender Norms in Turkish Society and the Gülen Movement

In order to interpret women's choices, comments, and the answers these provide to feminist critiques, we must know the basic ideas about gender and possible lives for women that have developed along with all other aspects of the Gülen movement in the context of Turkish history (Turam 2000; Yavuz and Esposito 2003). Encouraging women's equal rights and visibility in public positions has enabled both the Turkish government and the Gülen movement to demonstrate they are modern in Europe-oriented definitions (Bozdoğan and Kasaba 1997; Turam 2000; White 2002). Turkey's 1926 institution of a civil code and continuing reforms emphasized women's rights in court, suffrage, inheritance of property, education, employment, and family life (Arat 1998). M. K. Atatürk, head of state in the newly formed republic, stated, "Turkish women shall be free, enjoy education, and occupy a position equal to that of men as they are entitled to" (Turam 2000:258). Especially for women in upwardly mobile classes, the republican revolution "ma[d]e for a liberal aura and allowed women to enter public life as professionals, writers,

133

and activists" (Arat 1998:8). Gülen's vision for women is based in Islam and shares similarities with that of Atatürk (Turam 2000). Gülen's support of Islamist women's education, employment, and world travel encourages the possibility for them to attain the best education and go on to public professions.

However, women's education and visibility in professional positions can be merely a token of equality rather than an outcome of true equal opportunity to use their talents toward personal growth and economic security as well as leadership in developing a Muslim worldview. Other beliefs in the Gülen movement and Turkish society that women's primary role is as nurturers cause women dilemmas in taking advantage of professional employment or being in leadership. For example, Atatürk also said the following:

> The duty of the Turkish woman is raising generations that are capable of preserving and protecting the Turk with his mentality, strength and determination. The woman who is the source and social foundation of the nation can fulfill her duty only if she is virtuous. [Arat 1998:1]

Based on interpretations of the Qur'an, and the Hadith, Gülen also speaks of women's God-given role as compassionate, educated mothers who rear the next generation of a strong Turkish nation:

> Women train and educate children, and establish order, peace, and harmony in the home. They are the first teachers in the school of humanity. At a time when some are in search of a new place for them in society, we would like to remind them once again of the unique position God bestowed upon them. [Ünal and Williams 2000:136]

On the other hand, men are considered intrinsically suited to leadership. The ideal for a man in Turkey and the movement often remains the professionally employed financial provider and keeper of the worldview who displays authority, intelligence, and a less emotional personality.

Many women inspired by the Gülen movement feel they can best serve their nation and God in low-paid or unpaid roles such as mothers, volunteers, and teachers (Turam 2000). Even so, they often enjoy the level of status common for women in upwardly-mobile social classes rather than the subservience more common in lower-class Islamist homes (White 2002). Yet, statistics show opportunities through professional work are essential for women's true and sustained status (Kagitcibasi 1986). As experienced by women around the world, attempting to fulfill both expectations as primary nurturers and as professionals can lead to the burden of the "superwoman syndrome." As a woman in Turkey associated with the Gülen movement explained to me:

> Society has an attitude that no matter what your accomplishments are in life you are to care for your house as a beloved wife and caring mother. You get your education and then marry not too late or too early. You work outside the home, but be home before your husband to have a clean house and good hot meals. This is superwoman!

Projects of building modern nations around the world have often called for, "both women's greater participation in the public world—through education, unveiling, and political participation—and women's enormous responsibility for the domestic sphere" (Abu-Lughod 1998:8).

Inequality also arises when women who choose to work professionally do not have power in public places. Although women do work in the movement's media, business, and education enterprises, they do not necessarily share equally in high positions, generally do not take part in official religious interpretation, and often look to men's authority (Turam 2000).[1]

Women and men in the Gülen movement often maintain a level of separation for purity, which can result in the absence of women from men's leadership activities (Turam 2000). Separation can also entail the option of covering (wearing a headscarf and modest dress) for women. Serious resistance from secularists and Islamists to covered women holding positions in public places has further limited women who choose to cover from taking professional or powerful positions in society. Muslim women who opt to cover have resisted this limitation by informal methods with some success (Göle 2003).

---

[1] Many men in the Gülen movement also work in beneficial but lower paying professions as philanthropists and teachers and are not in a position to contribute at a high level to the movement's worldview. Further study is needed to understand the relationship between men's and women's status in the movement.

In conclusion, many middle- and upper-class women in Turkey, including those of the Gülen movement, are able to obtain the highest levels of education. Many are visible in professions. However, ambivalences in gender beliefs and norms lead to the conclusion that the Turkish state and the Gülen movement still "equat[e] women's equality and liberation with women's public visibility instead of creating specific channels to women's equality and emancipation" (Turam 2000:275). According to Turam's research, most women in the movement rationalize and support their "subordinated agency" instead of questioning and challenging it (Turam 2000:289).

Women in Houston Question and Legitimize Gender Norms

At the time of this study, similar beliefs about gender separation, men's role as leaders and financial providers, and women's primary role as nurturers had led to similar outcomes among Gülen movement participants in Houston. Men were largely recognized as leaders of the community's educational endeavors, cultural foundation, and interfaith dialogue institute. Women were active as students, mothers, volunteers, teachers, or in professions outside the movement's cooperative activities. In response to the critique that women in the movement support limits to professional goals and leadership opportunities, life histories from Gülen movement participants in Houston give examples of those who informally resisted the limiting potential of some gender beliefs while they rationalized others. Their awareness of limitations was primarily informed by sources outside the movement such as personal experiences, media, university attendance, and examples of women they look up to in society. Their ways of negotiating around limits were informed by sources outside as well as inside the movement. In the following examples I highlight stories from early adulthood when identity-defining decisions such as education, marriage, and career were made. I edited the following stories for clarity and conciseness. Contributors reviewed them to ensure my representations reflected their realities, as an important aspect of qualitative methodology.

One informant had lived in Houston for two years. Her home in Turkey embraced "traditional" gender beliefs, but gradually accepted some liberal ideas evolving in middle-class society toward women. For example, she was the first woman in her family to attend university, as were most of my informants.

> I wanted to go to university because I wanted to be free; to move out of my small town, to make my own money. It was never my aim to be rich or to buy whatever I want, but I didn't want to be dependent on my parents or worry in the future. I didn't want to have to be dependent on my husband for finances, either. I saw how relationships sometimes don't work out and women aren't free to change the situation.

She recognized problems arise from gender norms in which women are financially dependent on parents or a husband. Her motivations for education were social mobility, material security, and independence. After being influenced by Gülen's teachings she "realized we should leave 'footprints' behind us in this life; do something that makes an improvement. Not just live for yourself, to be rich, have a bachelor or master's degree to your name." Helping others as a use of her talents appealed to this informant. However, she did not renounce her goals of self-actualization and independence. She fulfilled all of these motives by traveling outside Turkey and working in the movement. Later, she continued to fulfill them by moving from teaching at a Gülen-inspired school in Eastern Europe to studying in a graduate program in Houston.

> After four years, teaching high school became monotonous and I wanted a change of location. I was ready to get my master's degree, and my husband was encouraging me. We decided to apply in America, because it's obvious this is the best place to have a masters or any graduate level study. My husband came to America before we were together and he loved it. Besides, it's not logical for me to live in Turkey now. There is the problem of wearing a scarf and working.[2]

She described her motives for moving as, first, simply not being satisfied as a high school teacher. Second, she had the option to obtain high quality education and took that opportunity. Third, she could become a university professor; in other words, she could move to the next level in her career where she could be more intellectually challenged (and incidentally

---

[2] Teachers in Turkey are not permitted to cover their hair while working in a school, whether public or private.

137

have access to higher economic gain and contribution to the world of ideas as an academic). Pre-established networks and a supportive husband informed and facilitated her choice to move to Houston to continue her career path.

In Houston, with a husband who is very busy in community work, responsibility for home life rested on her. She purposely attempted to avoid this dilemma by choosing a husband open-minded to sharing responsibility for home care and childcare while both parents held careers. However, life cannot always be predicted. In Houston she did not have access to quality childcare or domestic help as she would have had in Turkey or at the school where she used to work. She relied on a friend to watch her child, but it was not a permanent arrangement and created ongoing concern. Childcare was an important factor in her decision whether nor not to go on for her Ph.D. at that time.

> I looked at daycares, but I didn't like what was available in my financial range. I don't want to be a stay at home mom, but making money is not worth it for me to put a child in a day care of low standards. I could stay at home until my child goes to school and then continue my education. But it might be difficult to get started in a program again.

Yet, she sought the best childcare possible in order to satisfy her intellectual interests by going on for a Ph.D. In her work at the university she discovered another opportunity to leave her footprints behind in professional work.

> Now that I am lecturing at university, I can show that as a Muslim woman, choosing to cover my head with a scarf doesn't mean that I'm not modern or capable as a professional. For example my students didn't know what to think of me at the beginning of this semester because they have never had a teacher wearing a scarf. But some of them ended up appreciating my teaching so much that I believe I changed their negative opinions about Muslims. I believe more and more that what I do is really important. I am leaving footprints behind me in this world, and I hope they get bigger as time passes.

In summary, this informant was conscious of limits to her self-determination and career goals that could be caused not only by stereotypes of covered Muslim women but also by the view that men are leaders and financial providers while women are nurturers. She attempted to negotiate limits to her career and independence by partnering with a husband open-minded to sharing home responsibilities and professional aspirations, studying and working in the United States, having a small family, keeping a modest home, and utilizing childcare. She also interpreted Mr. Gülen's ideas in ways that supported her goals and identity. She said, "Mr. Gülen says women must get educated, work, and have power in society" as opposed to focusing on life as a stay at home mom or volunteer. She was motivated to resist and negotiate limits by the desire to set an example for the benefit of Muslims in the public space and create positive change in society as well as by her identity as a modern, intellectual, and independent woman.

A second informant had lived in Houston for almost a decade. She grew up in a secular home where her mother influenced her desire for a career, which to her was an important part of being a modern woman.

> My mother…is a very outgoing and strong person and liked working outside the home. I got my ambition from her. I was a very modern girl. I wanted to work, and I was planning to do lots of things. Attending class was not enough for me in business school. I made an internship for myself, which was not common in Turkey. I could do things in my field better than most other colleagues, because I worked to be competitive. I was planning to have my master's degree in Europe or the United States. In Turkey parents pay for education. Mine couldn't, so I applied for scholarships and worked.

Studying in the United States was a goal; however, it was an unexpected family need for medical treatment that actually brought her to Houston. During that hard time she became interested in religion to make sense of life. She also met a practicing Turkish-Muslim man studying at a Houston university who became her husband. He was on a path toward material success and was supportive of her goals to pursue a master's degree and a career in business. At that time she also chose to make a substantial change to her public identity by covering. She knew this invited career limits but believed society's negative perception of covered women would change over time. She went on to pursue a master's degree in finance in Houston and returned with her family to Turkey. Through these experiences, the superwoman syndrome began to take its toll on her.

> I thought my time in the United States was limited, so I pushed to finish my master's degree even through a high-risk pregnancy. After we finished our degrees and returned to Turkey, I took care of everything at home while my husband served his military duty. I

139

really wanted to work, but I couldn't work in my field, tourism, because I was now wearing a scarf. No one in that field would hire someone wearing a scarf. Also, it was hard to find someone who would take care of the children.

Another family member's illness brought her back to Houston, where she would have likely been able to move forward in her desired career.

I was still very frustrated about not working, even though I was putting so much energy into helping with my child's treatment. I expected so much from my life, I think. A psychologist thought I should continue working at all costs. But after some time, trying to do it all didn't make me happy. Now, I don't have that much energy for performance. I used to ask, "Why does Islam suggest women not work outside as much?" But now I ask, "What was I doing all those years?"

She was very conscientious about benefiting society after becoming inspired by Gülen's ideas. However, her identity and life expectations were still oriented toward having a professional career, which social discourses link with prestige and modernity. Self-expectations can become overwhelming when professional goals are added to being a highly involved mother and community volunteer. She was concerned about this problem for her daughter in the future. However, she felt having experiences outside the home are important to developing self-esteem and future opportunities.

I want my daughter to experience many things. I want her to believe in herself and feel strong for herself. I take her to gymnastics, computer camp, basketball camp, and art school. But after she gets married, she may not have that many opportunities to be out all the time [due to responsibilities in the home]. She will still expect to be outside the home because she got used to it. She has to know there are different situations. So I'm not sure what the balance is.

This informant recognized a problem in the outcome but did not find fault in the Gülen movement's gender beliefs. On the other hand, she was aware that there is a problem with men's lack of nurturing involvement in the family beyond financial provision. She accepted much responsibility for raising their children, but still worked seriously in everyday encounters to increase her husband's involvement in a nurturing role.

He doesn't have a tendency to spend a lot of time with kids because his father didn't. But I could tell the children needed him.

I told him when they asked about him or what they said about him every day. We would visit him at work every day, even for five minutes. One day when we couldn't visit, he asked, "Where were you? I missed you." So he has become more and more involved with them. And he is happier too. When you have felt close to your children, you always want to keep that good feeling.

She felt men's nurturing input in family life is important to raise a psychologically sound generation and provide a new model for family relationships in the next generation. Life experiences also taught her that sharing more home duties with their husbands could make it easier for women to be engaged professionally.

Not all women inspired by the Gülen movement feel their best work is done in volunteer, low-paid, or low-profile positions. However, burn-out can keep them from fulfilling their career dreams and their identity as intellectual, professional women. The two informants whose stories are written above were involved in a formal group discussion in which I heard several women question ideas about gender resulting in the superwoman syndrome. Participants highly valued the role of mother, yet they explored variations in the importance of their ability to pursue career goals and fathers' roles in raising families. Career-minded women dealt with this dilemma by having few children, finding flexible jobs such as teaching, or waiting to marry while pursuing a career and volunteer work. Many consciously sought marriage with a man willing to assist in household duties and childcare while both husband and wife fulfill career ambitions. Like other women in Turkey, they saw gender roles more and more as including men and women working together in careers and family life. Others stayed home when children were small then went back to work later.

The discussion revolved around the question, "What can women contribute to society?" The first comment was, "Being a good mother to raise a good generation is women's major contribution to society. This has a chain reaction to affect all other aspects of society." A working woman countered with, "It doesn't matter whether a person is a man or a woman. Just being a good person is the most important thing anyone can do to affect society and help people." Others brought up the problem of building a career and being solely responsible for duties at home. One woman said:

> If I lived at Prophet Muhammad's time, I wouldn't worry about being in a career and taking care of everything in the house

141

because he was sharing in house responsibilities and was never demanding. Everyone is responsible for each other's happiness.

Another also attributed the problem to culture instead of religion; "There is no problem in Islam with men and women doing equal work [in the house]. It is in Turkish culture that the inequality arises." Another woman reported that her husband said, "The female bird builds the nest." She thought, "No, you share building of the home." She has successfully worked to get him involved in nurturing their children. All agreed that women create problems for themselves because they want freedom from the stereotypical dominant husband but also are attracted to a "man's man" idealized in culture (stable, not emotional, strong, more intelligent than those around him, hardworking, and financially successful).

These women viewed society and religious texts as supportive of women in professional roles as well as men in nurturing roles. However, they also agreed on the need to justify their working outside the home. Those who worked in fields such as medicine, academia, and technology said utilizing their talent, fulfilling personal dreams, and contributing to society motivated them. They did not speak of being motivated primarily by financial gain or by hopes of contributing to development of a different Muslim worldview. In this way women legitimized gender beliefs when negotiating possible limitations. They worked professionally, even in well-paying or prestigious careers, without challenging men's role as primary providers and natural leaders. Also, not working primarily for financial gain and working in white-collar professions did not go against the vision of pious women who keep themselves from materialistic dealings or rough environments.

Conclusions and Ongoing Questions

Gender beliefs and norms among the participants in the Gülen movement in Houston were consistent with wider cultural and religious ambivalence toward women's equal opportunities in professional and leadership roles. My informants' stories and comments provide examples of women who rationalized some limiting norms and did not necessarily seek leadership in the community's cooperative endeavors or in development of an Islamic worldview. However, their comments and stories also show they recognized, discussed, negotiated, and explored alternatives to some limiting status quo gender beliefs. They did so selectively and informally rather than by methodical analysis or official calls for change. They did not find limiting gender beliefs originated in Islam but rather saw the trouble as coming from incorrect religious interpretations or Turkish cultural norms. This is a common answer to the Gülen movement's other concerns. They interpreted Gülen's writings, the Qur'an, and the Hadith as promoting women's use of their talents professionally and in leadership, sharing home responsibilities with men, and men's potential for nurturing.

Women demonstrated awareness of limits due to gender beliefs but were often conflicted as to whether and how to overcome them. They considered informal private action an important means to bring about change in society at large as advocated in the Gülen movement. This approach was applied consciously and unconsciously when negotiating gender stereotypes in personal and professional life choices, as well. They were motivated to do so by self-actualization, the movement's mission to show Islam as applicable in modern society, and in some cases by a desire to see changes in gender norms.

Ongoing research can monitor the effects of women's informal resistance to limits. More stories from women who are equipped intellectually and spiritually for leadership but also see nurturing of family and philanthropic volunteerism as important means to benefit society may yield insight into the balance of maximizing talents that is being sought by women around the world. Interpretation of men's life histories can also provide deeper insight into gender issues affecting the movement. Further study within the Gülen movement in the United States may demonstrate whether gender beliefs are affected by American discourses on gender norms, marriage with Americans, more prestigious career options for covered women, and the multicultural setting, where Muslim practices can be reinforced as part of Turkish identity.

The growing number of participants in Houston's Gülen movement is a part of the movement's inspiring humanitarian efforts to bring tolerance and understanding to our shared world. However, because the movement is becoming a global example of a Muslim community in modern society, it will continue to be scrutinized concerning women's equal opportunity in professional, social, and religious leadership. Although this complex issue has not been entirely resolved even in supposedly progressive societies, feminists and other social scientists will examine the movement not only for the token numbers of women in leadership and professions but also for attitudes and gender norms that make women's equal status and contribution at all levels a natural and obvious occurrence. Contributors to my research believed the movement is now young and attitudes toward gender are still emerging, therefore current increased educational and professional expectations of women will lead to consistent leadership roles for them within the movement and wider society. However, they can expect studies also to look for women themselves to formally insist on changes.

Women and Their Rights:
Fethullah Gülen's Gloss on Lady Montagu's "Embassy" to the Ottoman Empire

Bernadette Andrea

In one of the interviews collected in Advocate of Dialogue (Ünal and Williams 2000:139), *Hocaefendi* (esteemed teacher) Fethullah Gülen cites "the wife of an English ambassador" who traveled throughout the Ottoman Empire during the early eighteenth century as exemplary in her accurate understanding of the rights for women as established in the Qur'an. Lady Mary Wortley Montagu, who accompanied her husband on his embassy to the Ottoman court from 1716–18, learned that women under Islamic law could own property, could stipulate provisions in their marriage contract, and could ensure their privacy even from their husbands.[1] None of these rights were available to English women until the end of the nineteenth century, after which they continued to be contested.[2] Gülen's citation of Montagu, the remarkable woman who challenged the West's distorted view of Islam with

---

[1] For the application of Islamic law in the Ottoman Empire during the eighteenth century, see Zilfi 1997:28–47, 81–104, and 105–27.

[2] According to the eighteenth-century jurist William Blackstone, "by marriage the very being or legal existence of a woman is suspended, or at least it is incorporated or consolidated into that of the husband, under whose wing, protection and cover she performs everything, and she is therefore called in our law a *feme covert*" (Holcombe 1983:25). This absence of rights for English women continued until parliament passed the Married Women's Property Rights Acts in 1870 and 1882. However, married women in jurisdictions influenced by English traditions could not hold bank accounts, take out loans, or have credit cards in their own names until the 1970s (Women's history in America).

145

particular reference to gender, relates fundamentally to his abiding goal to promote dialogue between different cultural and religious groups, starting within Turkey during the 1990s and currently extending around the globe. Yet, one of the primary obstacles to this dialogue, despite Montagu's interventions in the eighteenth century, remains the West's distorted view of the rights and roles of Muslim women. As Leila Ahmed documents, the "Western narrative" from Montagu's era onwards maintains that "Islam was innately and immutably oppressive to women, that the veil and segregation epitomized that oppression, and that these customs were the fundamental reasons for the general and comprehensive backwardness of Islamic societies" (Ahmed 1992:149, 151–52). However, as Sherif Abdel Azeem Mohamed establishes in his study "Women in Islam versus Women in the Judaeo-Christian Tradition" (1995) and as Montagu knew from personal experience, the Judeo-Christian tradition followed literally disadvantaged women to a far greater degree than did the Islamic.[3] The West's distorted view of women and their rights according to the Qur'an thus functions not only to prevent interfaith dialogue due to inimical stereotypes, but also presents particular dangers to Western women who fall into these fallacies. More than once, women of Judeo-Christian backgrounds seduced by a false sense of superiority over Muslim women have been steadily deprived of their corresponding rights (Ahmed 1992:153).

In this paper, I pursue a dialogic analysis by considering Gülen's responses to questions about women and their rights from an Islamic perspective alongside Montagu's perception of Muslim women's rights during her travels throughout the Ottoman Empire. This analysis seeks to correct the stereotypical tendencies of Western discourses on Islam, including mainstream Western feminist discourses; it also expands the challenge to the accretion in Muslim communities of customs that have compromised the full expression of women's rights according to the Qur'an. Finally, in the spirit of Montagu's quest for accurate knowledge about Islam in assessing her own tradition, this analysis turns to the limits of the Judeo-Christian framework for women's rights. Ultimately, I hope this dialogue across cultures and centuries between Gülen and Montagu will yield a historicized analysis of

---

[3] The reprint of this article in *The Fountain,* a journal produced by Gülen's followers, does not include the epilogue from the original, which condemns the deviation in practice throughout the current Muslim world from the rights and status for women established by the Qur'an.

gender able to promote the rights for women which both these exemplars advocated.

Fethullah Gülen on the Rights of Women

As Thomas Michel affirms, Fethullah Gülen has emerged at the forefront of a movement for "[i]nterreligious dialogue," and more broadly a *dialogue of civilizations*," based on the principles of love, tolerance, and peace at the root of Islam (Michel 2004:i). As a respected teacher, preacher, and public figure for over four decades in his native Turkey, Gülen broke through numerous barriers to initiate discussions between otherwise separate religious and secular communities, first within Turkey and subsequently extending globally (Saritoprak and Griffith 2005). In addition to inspiring independent foundations, schools, and mass media based on these principles, Gülen continues to write prolifically about contemporary issues from an Islamic perspective. For instance, he addresses women's rights, which has taken center stage in the so-called "clash of civilizations," in numerous essays and interviews.[4] The controversy surrounding this issue has come from two sources in recent history: (1) the orientalist misrepresentation of all Muslim women as oppressed due to their religion, a view which gained force during the Western European colonial occupations from the nineteenth century onwards, and (2) the contemporaneous resurgence of what has been called "Islamic fundamentalism," which like other fundamentalisms selectively deploys religious texts to enforce confining and discriminatory policies against women.[5] Gülen responds to both tendencies by drawing on his firm foundation as an "intellectual-ulama" or thoroughly trained scholar who seeks the fundamentals of Islam in a holistic reading of the Qur'an, with support from the Prophet's Sunna, rather than in subsidiary commentaries or customs (Bulaç 2005:199; Tuncer 2006). His extensive education in the traditional Islamic sciences thus renders him an authority in a manner many

---

[4] Gülen (2004d:255–57) categorically rejects the "clash of civilizations" thesis, elaborated most controversially by Samuel Huntington.

[5] I use the term "fundamentalism" with caution, since this politicization of religion encompasses major religions such as Christianity, Judaism, and Hinduism, along with Islam. For an examination of Gülen's teachings as a tool to challenge Christian fundamentalism, see Ashton (2005). For a wide-ranging analysis of "Islamic fundamentalism" or "Islamism" that establishes Gülen's rejection of these political ideologies, see Barton (2005).

modern pronouncers on Islam, often with dangerous consequences, are not.[6] Moreover, his openness to currents in Western literary, philosophic, religious, and scientific thought renders his message more accessible to a diverse global audience. Since the 1990s, in particular, Gülen's views have been disseminated to Western, and especially English-speaking, audiences via the internet and international publishing ventures.

My sources for assessing Gülen on the rights of women consist of articles and interviews translated from Turkish to English drawn from archives on his website and from published collections of his writings. These sources represent the sum of Gülen's views currently accessible to an English-speaking audience and should be supplemented by scholars conversant with Gülen's complete works in Turkish.[7] Nevertheless, because one of Gülen's goals is interfaith and intercultural dialogue, a focus on his writings translated for an English-speaking audience is warranted when assessing his intervention into current debates about the status of women, not only in the Muslim context but in the Judeo-Christian as well. Hence, I am interested in the ideals Gülen enunciates, which he presents as Qur'anic, rather than their implementation or lack thereof in Muslim communities, including those defining themselves as Gülen's followers. Several sociological studies have suggested Gülen's ideals may not be completely practiced in these communities. Only further field research can determine if this is indeed the case. [8]

Gülen's views on the rights of women were first translated for an English-speaking audience in the collection *Pearls of Wisdom* (2000a). Using an aphoristic style, Gülen focuses on women's traditional position as the first educators of their children and as those charged with "establish[ing] order, peace, and harmony in the home." He continues, "at a time when some are in

---

[6] Such as Osama bin Laden, whom Gülen deems defective in Islamic understanding (2004c:217–19; 2004a).

[7] For instance, Gülen's mentioning of Rabi'a Adawiyye [or Basri] as a leading Sufi figure in various sermons is not yet accessible to a non-Turkish-speaking audience. My thanks to the Editorial Committee for the Second International Conference on Islam in the Contemporary World for drawing my attention to this reference. Also see Smith (1997).

[8] Yavuz (2003b:29) observes that "Gülen himself...is more practical and progressive than his community." For interviews of women in the Gülen movement within Turkey, see Özdalga (2003), and as immigrants to the United States, see Stephenson (2006).

search of a new place for them in society, we would like to remind them once again of the unique position God bestowed upon them" (Gülen 2000a:52). Gülen additionally addresses the use of women as "objects of pleasure, means of entertainment, and material for advertising," which he deplores. He rejects the focus on external beauty, exhorting women to focus on "the road .of immortality." Implicitly, he also addresses men who are prone to focus on externals, instead counselling them to turn their "familiar looks" to "instinctive feelings of contemplation" for what is immortal as expressed through the wisdom, delicacy, and refinement of his ideal woman. Hence, Gülen rejects the patriarchal logic that men's desire is women's fault. He is firm in asserting daughters should be deemed "very valuable," and he suggests this valuing of women should be extended beyond the family into society (Gülen 2000a:53). Yet, Gülen remains critical of modern "champions of women's rights and freedoms" who reduce such liberty to sexual license, as in the 1960s and 1970s in the United States (Gülen 2000a:54). Western feminists themselves have cast a critical eye on this conflation of liberty with license, noting such "rights" served mostly to extend males' access to women while relieving men of their traditional responsibilities. However, feminists, not only in the West, have guarded against the opposite extreme of barring women from the public sphere in response to such excesses. With many women claiming their "Islamic right" to be educated and to earn a living, this early essay consequently begs questions as to what degree does Gülen support this resurgent movement and to what degree does he adhere to traditions that would confine women to the home.[9]

While Gülen's stance regarding women's roles outside the home remains ambiguous in this early essay, elsewhere he specifies, "although it is fundamental that girls be brought up to be delicate like flowers and mild and affectionate educators of children, due attention must be given to making them inflexible defenders of truth. Otherwise, we shall have transformed

---

[9] Cooke defines "Islamic feminism" as the recourse of Muslim women to their rights through a non-patriarchal interpretation of the Qur'an, which means the rejection of a definition of women's rights (or restrictions) via the corpus of medieval commentaries or entrenched customs (2001:ix-xvii). An "Islamic feminist" contrasts in this sense with a secular feminist, who feels she must reject religion in order to achieve gender justice. Samples of this resurgent movement include the writings of women and men, such as Engineer (1992), Wadud (1999), al-Disuqi (1999), and Barlas (2002). For a critique of the "Islamic feminist" label as too narrow, see Abugideiri 2001:18 n. 36.

them into poor, impotent beings for the sake of delicacy and mildness." Explicitly asserting the fundamental equality of males and females, Gülen concludes: "we must not forget that female lions are still lions" (Ünal and Williams 2000:310). Even more tellingly, at a 1995 Ramadan dinner in Istanbul, to which only "a small number of women had been invited," Gülen made a point of encouraging Professor Nur Vergin and journalist Nuriye Akman to give "short speeches." In addition, Gülen "called Nur Vergin to his table from her seat at a table of journalists." The report on this dinner states that not all the women were "covered" (i.e., dressed in *hijab*, with a headscarf covering the hair and neck and loose clothing covering the body), and some were "strikingly dressed." As the reporter notes, "just as this [recognition of women in the public sphere] led to an increased attack against Fethullah Hoca in *Cuma*'s latest issue, it was also perceived as a challenge to Islamic groups that don't share his views on women" (Onal 1995). Ultimately, Gülen's commitment is to the truth of Islam, based fundamentally in the Qur'an, rather than to "feminism" as such. However, if, as recent writers on women and Islam have claimed, the Prophet Muhammad's immense respect for women and unwavering commitment to their rights may be seen as "feminist" in the most basic sense, then perhaps Gülen's views are more complex than his early essay on Women suggests.[10]

Gülen's subsequent statements on women's rights come almost entirely in response to questions from interviewers, though he has published some essays on polygamy related to the overall issue.[11] In a 1997 interview, subsequently published in *Advocate of Dialogue* (Ünal and Williams 2000), he was asked about contemporary pressures to "separate men and women in

---

[10] Hasan (2000:124) asserts that "the Prophet Muhammad was one of the world's first feminists and that Islam is a feminist's religion." Nomani (2005:198) references Hasan when affirming "the prophet was Islam's first feminist." The term *feminist*, which was coined at the end of the nineteenth century is not necessarily amenable to cross-cultural application. Indeed, it is anachronistic when applied to Montagu. The focus on women's rights may be more apt, though when the term *feminist* is used in this essay it is in its basic sense, which is synonymous with Gülen's concern with the rights of women.

[11] Gülen's discussions of polygamy focus primary on Prophet Muhammad, defending him against Western aspersion. Regarding current arguments for polygamy, Gülen concludes that "if polygamy is considered as a stain on Islam and causes people to turn away from Islam, a Muslim does not have the right to practice it" and that "no one can consider marrying four women a matter of fulfilling a *sunna*; they can't claim to have fulfilled any religious law by doing so" (Ünal and Williams 2000:143–44).

society and in places of worship," which the interviewer felt contradicted earlier Islamic practices, particularly in a Turkish context. Gülen concurs, "women and men prayed together in mosques during the time of the Prophet," meaning women were not barred from mosques, though men and women did not pray shoulder to shoulder (Ünal and Williams 2000:139). As he elaborates, while women may be exempted if they so choose from "perform[ing] their prescribed prayers in mosques," they "should not be banned if there is no justifiable reason for banning them." In other words, he refutes the faulty logic that exemption, initially motivated by consideration for women who had childrearing responsibilities, constitutes exclusion, which would be an unwarranted discriminatory practice against all women. He supports this conclusion by adding an account from the time of the Caliph 'Umar, when a woman in the congregation challenged the Caliph's interpreting a particular verse of the Qur'an to the financial detriment of women. Famously, the Caliph admitted he had "'erred, and the woman spoke the truth.'" Gülen concludes this interview by stressing his concern, which he repeats elsewhere, that "secondary issues," such as barring women from mosques or requiring them to cover their heads, have overshadowed the core requirements of Islam, starting with the five pillars of the witnessing to God's oneness and the Prophet's message, prescribed prayer, fasting during Ramadan, the payment of zakat in charity, and pilgrimage to Mecca if possible (Ünal and Williams 2000:140).[12]

Elsewhere Gülen was asked even more pointed questions about women's rights and roles in the public sphere. He begins by establishing the reciprocity between man and woman based on his reading of the Qur'an: "Man without woman, or woman without man cannot exist; they were created together." Hence, "Man and woman complement each other" (Ünal and Williams 2000:138).[13] In *The Messenger of God: Muhammad* (2005a), Gülen states his view even more strongly:

---

[12] Nomani (2005:205) records how some "American mosque leaders" "tried to rationalize discrimination through a hadith: 'Do not prevent your women from [going to] the mosques, though their houses are best for them.' Scholars consider this hadith an allowance, not a restriction. The prophet made the statement after women, busy with household chores, complained when he said Muslims get twenty-seven times more blessing when praying at the mosque" (interpolation in the original).

[13] Here Gülen suggests that Adam preceded Eve in creation, a Judeo-Christian view that other Qur'anic interpreters contest (Ünal and Williams 2000:138; also 2005a:164; cf. Engineer

> Women are secondary beings in the minds of many,
> including those self-appointed defenders of women's rights
> as well as many self-proclaimed Muslim men. For us, a
> woman is part of a whole, a part that renders the other half
> useful. We believe that when the two halves come together,
> the true unity of a human being appears. When this unity
> does not exist, humanity does not exist—nor can
> Prophethood, sainthood, or even Islam. [Gülen 2005a:162]

Gülen acknowledges potential differences between men and women: for instance, "men usually are physically stronger and apt to bear hardship, while women have deeper emotions; they are more compassionate, more delicate, more self-sacrificing."[14] However, such differences should not become grounds for hierarchy. Again drawing on the Qur'an, Gülen confirms, "God created everything, from sub-atomic particles to human beings, in pairs to form a unity" (Ünal and Williams 2000:138). The radical nature of these claims for a Western audience, which are really claims from the Qur'an, can only be appreciated if we recall that in the Judeo-Christian tradition Eve is seen as derivative of Adam and the source of all evil as the instigator of the Fall (Genesis 3; 1 Timothy 2:11–15). One of Montagu's near contemporaries, the great seventeenth-century English poet John Milton, summarized the Western view in his epic poem, *Paradise Lost*, when he declared of Adam and Eve: "He for God only, she for God in him" (Book 4, line 299).[15] Such a view, which formed the basis of discriminatory cultural, legal, religious, and social practices against women in the West for centuries, runs completely contrary to Gülen's model of equality in complementarity, which is based in the Qur'an.

1992:42–43; Stowasser 1994:25–38; Wadud 1999:19–20; al-Disuqi 1999:7–8; Barlas 2002: 40, 135–39).

[14] For a Western feminist view that resonates with Gülen's, see Gilligan (1982). Gilligan "came to be known as the founder of 'difference feminism.' Many feminists insisted that there are no differences between males and females. Gilligan asserted that women have differing moral and psychological tendencies than men. According to Gilligan, men think in terms of rules and justice and women are more inclined to think in terms of caring and relationships. She asks that Western society begin to value both equally" (Women's intellectual contributions). For the "sameness versus difference" debate in Western feminism, see Hirsh (1990) and Andrew (2005).

[15] Milton first published this epic poem, considered the greatest in the English language, in 1667, with an expanded definitive edition published in 1671. *Paradise Lost* remained influential into the twentieth century.

Moreover, Gülen's assessment of the differences between men and women runs counter to a second discriminatory tradition in the West: the authoritative classical Greek legacy epitomized by the philosopher Aristotle.[16] Aristotle opined that women were "imperfect men," hence incomplete beings inherently subject to subordination and enslavement. Moreover, his hierarchy hinged on the association of reason with men, and emotion, deemed an inferior quality, with women. Gülen does not reproduce this hierarchical model of gender difference, instead specifying that in general greater physical strength characterizes men and in general deeper emotions, such as compassion, characterize women. Such emotion, therefore, is not seen as weakness, as in the Aristotelian tradition, but as civilizing. Reason, moreover, is not exclusively men's province, but is shared by the human pair. In response to questions about "the female role," Gülen further clarifies: "in the social atmospheres of Muslim societies where Islam is not 'contaminated' with customs or un-Islamic traditions, Muslim women are full participants in daily life" (Ünal and Williams 2000:138). Since the Islamic world of the Middle Ages shared in the classical Greek legacy, some of those contaminations are similar to those that have shaped the Western tradition. To counter these un-Islamic accretions, Gülen cites as a role model 'A'isha, one of the Prophet's wives, who "led an army" (more accurately translated as "was one of the leading figures" in the army) and "was a religious scholar whose views everyone respected."[17] He reiterates the point he made in an earlier interview that "women prayed in mosques together with men" and "an old woman could oppose the caliph in the mosque in a judicial matter." He finally responds, "there's no reason a woman can't be an administrator," and "Hanafi jurisprudence says that a woman can be a judge." It is in this interview that Gülen cites "the wife of an English ambassador" to the Ottoman Empire, who during the eighteenth century "highly praised the women and mentioned their roles in Muslim families and society with admiration" (Ünal and Williams 2000:139). This woman was Lady Mary

---

[16] Aristotle's influence also informed medieval Islamic exegesis, from which it was transmitted into the Western tradition and embedded into Christian theology through Thomas Aquinas (Peters 1968).

[17] My thanks to Muhammed Cetin, President of the Institute of Interfaith Dialog, for clarifying the language of this passage. Also see Abbott (1998).

Wortley Montagu, whose understanding of women's rights in her *Turkish Embassy Letters* I shall explicate in the next section of this essay.[18]

Gülen's most recent discussion stresses that he does not promote excluding women from specific roles: "The contribution of women in certain fields of life is not banned in Islam, provided the physical conditions have been taken into consideration and their working conditions are suitable." He reiterates, "women have indeed contributed in every field of life (throughout history). For instance, they were allowed to participate in battles; their education was not only desired, but actively sought and encouraged." Gülen cites many instances of such women, not restricting his examples to the Prophet's wives. He concludes, "In Islam, there is no such thing as limiting the life of women or narrowing their fields of activity." The restrictions on women in Muslim communities, he stresses, must be seen in light of customary practices and political agendas that are not necessarily Islamic. "Women," Gülen underscores, "can assume any role." However, his focus ultimately, for men as well as women, is on "ful[filling] their faith" rather than achieving worldly ends. Hence, "there may be some women who can fulfill their faith while employed in the public service, while others at home may fail in observing the faith fully." [19]

Gülen is categorical in asserting that women are not limited to—or, in the interviewer's terms, imprisoned in—the home. He also refutes the fallacy that women are inferior to men, which has marred the discourse of many traditional scholars, by reiterating difference does not mean hierarchy. As he points out, the four major Islamic schools of jurisprudence, which developed more than a century after the life of the Prophet, were shaped by "the culture of the time," wherein the expanding Muslim empires had incorporated the un-Islamic traditions of the Persian Sassanids and the Greek Byzantines, such as slave concubinage, seclusion of women in harems, and polygamy as a norm for upper-class men. Gülen even claims in some cases

---

[18] Other than a few incidental emendations, Jack's modernized edition of Montagu's *Turkish Embassy Letters* closely follows the first published version of *Letters of the Right Honourable Lady M---y W---y M----e: written, during her travels in Europe, Asia and Africa, to persons of distinction* (Dublin, 1763).

[19] For his part, Gülen, responding to charges that he engaged in political subversion, stresses that his "attention has never wavered from the ultimate goal of my life, i.e. searching for God" (Cetin, 2005:152).

women may be seen as superior to men, citing the praise of the Prophet for mothers over fathers and clarifying, once again, that the exemptions the Prophet established out of consideration for women did not mean they should be deprived of their equal access to places of worship, the ability to make a living, consent in marriage, and so on.

Regarding prayer, he emphasizes "full submission" to God is its raison d'être, which, as he clarifies in other interviews, does not mean women should be barred from mosques, but that both men and women should ensure their modesty in such contexts. Regarding the headscarf for women, particularly in the Turkish context in which women wearing *hijab* were barred from public universities, Gülen recalls his advice during this crisis that the education of women was most important, and that the headscarf is not a principle of the faith.[20] Gülen also provides an illuminating example, particularly in the present climate when Westerners tend to equate all instances of Islamic hijab with women's oppression, of his audience with Pope John Paul II, when a woman in his delegation was barred from the Vatican because "the Pope does not meet with women." As Gülen rightly remarks, if the Head of the Directorate of Religious Affairs in Turkey announced he "meets only men, he does not accept women . . . this would be headlines."

Yet, Gülen may be too sanguine in his assessment of the veil in the Christian tradition when he states, "if alternations had not happened in the essential sources of Christianity and if the clothing of women, like the nun's covering were mentioned in their present sources, they would not oppose the headscarf" (2005d). In reality, the connotations attached to women covering their heads are vastly different in the Christian and Islamic sources, with the Pauline letters specifying that women must cover their heads because they are derivative of men and the sources of all evil as daughters of Eve (1 Corinthians 11:3–10; 14:34–35). Such injunctions, which formed the basis of the household code in Western Christianity, resulted in centuries of oppression for women under Catholic and Protestant governments. By contrast, the source texts in the Qur'an that have been interpreted to account

---

[20] On the political circumstances surrounding the ban on headscarves in public institutions in Turkey, see Cetin 2005:147. Gülen discusses the headscarf issue in several interviews, though he does not do so in isolation from related questions about Islamic dress for men (Ünal and Williams 2000:62–64, 140–41; Yavuz 2003b:29).

for women's covering (whether that means "bosoms," as specified in Sura 24:31, or also the head, as implied by the use of the noun *khimar* or "head-covering") are not coded with similar denigrations of women as derivative or devils.

The first passage related to women's covering actually begins with the command to men to lower their eyes and remain chaste, before turning to women, using exactly the same language, as well as accounting for the erogenous quality of women's bosoms to apply additional advice. A modest society from a Qur'anic perspective, therefore, begins with men controlling their behavior and not, as some interpreters attempting to exclude women from the public sphere would have it, with the uncontrollable attractions of women. The second passage related to women's covering in the Qur'an focuses on protecting women in a context of extreme sexual harassment, which was perpetuated by the men of the *Jahiliyyah* (Age of Ignorance), some of whom were hypocritically claiming they were Muslim. In a truly Islamic society, this passage implies, women would not be subject to such harassment; hence, the phenomenon of moral "guardians," whether state sponsored or not, to compel women into compliance with strict dress codes seems to conform more to the practices of the age of ignorance. In summary, the fundamental message of the Qur'an is that every member of society should seek to be modest, both male and female, and that a society in which women are not harassed is ideal. Hence, hostility to *hijab* from Western women should be traced to the connotations of inferiority and subordination associated with veiling in the Pauline letters, which contrasts with the very different basis for women's covering articulated in the Qur'an.

Gülen's interview for *The Muslim World* (Sarıtoprak 2005), a prestigious academic journal focusing on Christian–Muslim relations, synthesizes his views on women's rights articulated over a decade and a half in print: "Woman is equal to man in the rights of freedom of religion, freedom of expression, freedom to live a decent life, and freedom of finance. Equality before the law, just treatment, marriage and founding a family life, personal life, privacy and protection are all among the rights of women. Her possessions, life and dignity are assured like that of men. Violation of any of these rights results in severe punishment." She is therefore ontologically equal, as well as "free and independent before the law." As for specifics, he adds that the stipulation regarding two women (really one woman, with the other to remind her) substituting for one man when testifying relates to "oral testimony with regard to financial matters and loans" and that this injunction does not apply to women alone, but to men who were inexperienced in financial matters during the Prophet's time, such as Bedouins. It should not be extended as a universal injunction that women cannot testify to legal matters, nor that they are worth half a man (Sarıtoprak 2005:464, 465).

To conclude my explication of Gülen's views on women's rights, I wish to return to an earlier essay, "The New Man and Woman," first published in Turkish in 1998 and translated into English as part of the collection, *Towards a Global Civilization of Love and Tolerance* (2004d). While in this essay Gülen does not address women's rights as such, it is significant, particularly for a Western audience, that he pairs "man and woman" consistently as he imagines his ideal human. For Gülen, "These new people will be individuals of integrity who, free from external influences, can manage independently of others;" "Truly independent of any worldly power, they will think and act freely, for their freedom will be in proportion to their servanthood to God;" "They will think, investigate, believe, and overflow with spiritual pleasure" (Gülen 2004d:81). In the balance of this essay, Gülen stresses such people consist of women and men equally. Such inclusive language has been one of the major achievements of Western feminists, who were able to institute this shift only in recent decades. Hence, it may come as a surprise to many Westerners that Gülen is following Qur'anic practice, instituted in the seventh century of the Christian era, in using gender-inclusive language. Indeed, it was in response to the question of one of the Prophet's wives, Umm Salama, that the revelation began to convey in unambiguous language the fundamental equality between men and women that stands as one of the central themes of the Qur'an (Sura 33:35).[21] Fethullah Gülen, in his commitment to returning to these sources, even when they conflict with traditions that sometimes stand as norms in Muslim communities today, therefore becomes a champion of women's rights by scrupulously following the path of the Prophet Muhammad.

---

[21] On Umm Salama's question, which inspired this revelation, see Barlas, 2002:20. Gülen also cites an occasion when the Prophet consulted Umm Salama on a matter crucial for the nascent Muslim community. As Gülen concludes, "In doing this, he taught Muslim men an important social lesson: There is nothing wrong with exchanging ideas with women on important matters, or on any matters at all" (Gülen 2005a:162). On consultation as an Islamic imperative, see Gülen 2005c:43–58, where he again mentions Umm Salama. Also see Nadvi 2003:55–66.

Mary Wortley Montagu's Turkish Embassy Letters

Having established Fethullah Gülen's views on women's rights, as expressed in a decade and a half of articles and interviews translated into English for a global audience, I wish to turn to "the wife of an English ambassador" he cites as exemplary for her broadminded quest to seek accurate information about Muslim women's status at a time when English (and other Western European) men regurgitated salacious images of "the harem." Prior to examining Montagu's Turkish Embassy Letters, however, I must briefly survey the primary events of her life in the context of her society to establish a point of reference for her challenge to patriarchal orientalist clichés. As with most English women of her time, who were "understood either married or to be married," the pivotal event in Montagu's life consisted of matrimony (Klein 1992:28). As an aristocratic woman, Montagu could expect to have no say in this matter. The English upper-class at the time deemed marriage to be a property transaction, whereby the father of the potential bride "sold" his daughter for gain (Montagu 1993:xi). Montagu felt the injustice of this system keenly, particularly when she learned the man her father had chosen for her without her knowledge or consent seemed, in her terms, "Hell itself " (Grundy 1999:46). Despite being barred from a formal education (as was the norm for English women in her era), she possessed an immense hunger for knowledge, an exceptionally quick wit, and a writing style praised by the luminaries of her day. The man she chose to marry against her father's wishes, therefore, was one she felt could be more amenable to her desire to expand her knowledge through education and travel.

This man, Edward Wortley Montagu, came from a rising middle-class family, and therefore lacked the property and pedigree an aristocratic father desired from his daughter's marriage. Edward and Mary therefore eloped. Though this decision expressed Montagu's desire for self-determination, which was completely denied by her society, it was disastrous to her financially. English common law, in diametrical opposition to the rights established for women in the Qur'an, deprived women upon marriage of all property rights, including the right to any wages they earned or any inheritance. A dowry in the English tradition, unlike the *mahr* established in the Qur'an, was transmitted from the father of the bride for exclusive use of the husband. The *mahr* constituted a radical gain for women's rights, as it is presented solely to the bride as a condition of the marriage and becomes her inalienable property. The English aristocracy sought loopholes to the liabilities for women in English common law by establishing trusts or "portions" for their daughters in competing jurisdictions. A woman who eloped with a man not of her father's choosing, however, would not qualify for the "portion" that would provide her with a modicum of financial security. Montagu was well aware her entire married life that she owned nothing, that her welfare was based entirely on her husband's largesse, and that even the heirloom jewelry she wished to bestow on her daughter was not hers to give but her husband's (Grundy 1999:558). This awareness of the liabilities women experienced under English law and custom, which could impoverish even privileged aristocratic women, made Montagu one of the first English feminists.

Some commentators have opined that Lady Mary wed the lower-status Montagu, who did become a rich and powerful politician and businessman, because his interest in the diplomatic service might enable her to fulfill her dream of traveling abroad, which was a standard part of a young male aristocrat's education but an impossibility for all but a very few English women. When her husband was assigned the position of "Ambassador Extraordinary to the Court of Turkey," she was ecstatic. This embassy threaded its way through the major cities of Germany and the Hapsburg Empire, which encompassed modern day Austria and Hungary (the latter acquired from the Ottomans between 1699 and 1737). She entered the Ottoman Empire in the regions of modern Serbia, where she discussed Arabic language and literature and debated the status of women with the urbane Achmet Bey. Her next stop at Sofia, now the capital of Bulgaria, was the scene of the most commented upon passage in Montagu's account: the Turkish bath scene (Montagu 1993:57–60). Montagu then travelled to Adrianople, and finally to the capital of the Ottoman Empire, Istanbul.

In a series of letters that modify her arguably exoticist Turkish bath scene, Montagu describes several visits to the personal quarters of high-ranking Ottoman ladies. These letters chart Montagu's developing understanding of Muslim women's rights. Ultimately, the positive assessment she made propelled her to reflect on the relative liabilities of her own tradition. The first of her new acquaintances, whom Montagu describes as "the Grand Vizier's lady," has been identified as the wife of Arnaud Khalit Pasha, "who had been in office since August 1716" (Montagu 1993:176 n. 166). Montagu's initial impressions of the Grand Vizier's wife included her clothing (she wore a modest "sable vest"), her graciousness (she presented

Montagu to "half a dozen of her friends with great civility"), and her character ("she seemed a very good woman, near fifty years old"). Montagu clearly expressed surprise at the simplicity of the lady's surrounding, indicating the Grand Vizier's wife "guessed at my thoughts and told me that she was no longer of an age to spend either her time or money in superfluities; that her whole expense was in charity, and her employment in praying to God." Montagu's surprise was occasioned, perhaps, by stereotypes of Eastern, and particularly Muslim, decadence circulated by previous travel writers, all of whom were male. It is therefore significant that she presents this counter-example, based on her own experience, of an upper-class Ottoman woman of great, though understated, piety. The lady's husband, moreover, is presented along with her as "entirely given up to devotion." This Grand Vizier, stresses Montagu, "never looks upon any other woman and, what is much more extraordinary, touches no bribes," including an attempted bribe from Edward Wortley Montagu (Montagu 1993:87).

By this point, Montagu can confidently reject all previous travelogues, exclusively by men, as full of falsehoods. Referring to the popular narrative by Jean Dumont, she writes:

> 'Tis a particular pleasure to me here to read the voyages to
> the Levant, which are generally so far removed from truth
> and so full of absurdities I am very well diverted with them.
> They never fail to give you an account of the women, which
> 'tis certain they never saw, and talking very wisely of the
> genius of men, into whose company they are never
> admitted, and very often describe mosques which they dare
> not peep into. [Montagu 1993:104][22]

She extends this scathing critique to other male travel writers, including the seventeenth-century English men Paul Rycaut and George Sandys (Montagu 1993:138, 145).[23] Montagu continues her praise of the Ottoman world she was coming to know in greater depth, endorsing its legal system: "I am also charmed with many points of the Turkish law, to our

---

[22] Dumont authored *Nouveau Voyage au Levant* (1694), which was translated into English in 1696. This travelogue went through four English editions by 1705.

[23] Rycaut authored *The Present State of the Ottoman Empire* (1667), *The History of the Turkish Empire from the Year 1623 to the Year 1677* (1680-79), and *The Present State of the Greek and Armenian Churches* (1679). Sandys authored *A Relation of a Journey Begun . . . 1610 . . . Containing a Description of the Turkish Empire, of Egypt, of the Holy Land, of the Remote Parts of Italy* (1615).

shame it be spoken, better designed and better executed than ours" (Montagu 1993:108). She also reiterates her praise of the Qur'an, whose translations into Western European languages she now understands as distorted by political and doctrinal animosity. Though in a previous letter she purveyed the incorrect notion that Paradise in the Islamic view is closed to women, in this letter she states "'tis certainly false, though commonly believed in our parts of the world, that Mohammed excludes women from any share in a future happy state" (Montagu 1993:109). Montagu presents, though perhaps tongue-in-cheek, a paradise in which wives are separated from their husbands, with the suggestion "the most part of them [the wives!] won't like it the worse for that."[24] Finally, when addressing women's exclusion from "affairs of state" or "the fatigues of war," Montagu stresses the Almighty, from the Ottoman Muslim perspective, "has entrusted them with an office which is not less honourable, even that of multiplying the human race" (Montagu 1993:110). Her tone becomes quite biting as she addresses her interlocutor, a Catholic priest, with this praise of motherhood over his church's privileging of lifelong celibacy.

Recounting another visit to a high-ranking Ottoman woman, "the Sultana Hafise, favourite of the last Emperor Mustafa [1695–1703]" (Montagu 1993:113), Montagu presents the Sultana as a paragon of virtue. Following the death of the Sultan, "she passes her time in uninterrupted mourning with a constancy very little known in Christendom" (Montagu 1993:114). The Sultana becomes Montagu's direct source to challenge the multiple stereotypes of the imperial harem promulgated by male travel writers: for instance, "she assured me that the story of the Sultan's throwing a handkerchief is altogether fabulous" (Montagu 1993:116).[25] In her next visit, this time returning to "the palace of my lovely friend, the fair Fatima" (Montagu 1993:118), Montagu employs a reverse gaze, as she had done earlier in the Turkish bath scene, whereby she becomes the object of scrutiny. In this case, Fatima remarks, "'You Christian ladies,' she said with a smile that

---

[24] Countering stereotypes of "Mahomet's paradise" as a place of sensual pleasures for males only, the Qur'an presents numerous descriptions of paradise inclusive of both female and male believers (Wadud 1999:44–61).

[25] According to Montagu's modern editor, "the reference is to an incident, recorded by [Paul] Rycaut, [*Present State of the Ottoman Empire* (1668)] in which the Grand Signor [Ottoman sultan] threw his handkerchief to one of the women in the Seraglio as a sign that she should come to his bed" (Montagu:1993:178 n. 225).

made her as handsome as an angel, 'have the reputation of inconstancy, and I did not expect, whatever goodness you expressed for me at Adrianople, that I should ever see you again.'" By the time of this return visit Montagu could "understand her [friend's] language," a testament to her commitment to learning firsthand about the Turkish culture in which she lived (Montagu 1993:119).

Importantly, as she becomes a more informed participant in Ottoman culture, Montagu refrains from presenting an unrealistically idealized representation of women's status. For instance, she records the discovery of a murdered woman, found "naked, only wrapped in a coarse sheet, with two wounds with a knife, one in her side and one another in her breast." As "no woman's face being known" outside her immediate family due to traditional veiling, no one could identify the victim (Montagu 1993:135).[26] Yet, in the same letter as this cautionary tale, she includes a story that suggests Muslims may be more desirable than Christians as husbands. She begins authoritatively: "I am well acquainted with a Christian woman of quality who made it her choice to live with a Turkish husband" (Montagu 1993:136). A Spanish woman captured by a Turkish Admiral, upon her family's rendering her ransom with the request that she return to be placed in a convent, demanded the Admiral marry her to restore her honor. She also demanded the entire ransom, which was substantial, for her "portion" or *mahr*. As Montagu records, the Admiral "married her [returning the ransom to her family and paying her *mahr* out of his own fortune] and never took any other wife and (as she says herself) she never had any reason to repent the choice she made." Moreover, Montagu suspects it wasn't just a matter of honor motivating the Spanish woman's marriage proposal, but this woman "might be reasonably touched at his generosity, which is very often found amongst Turks of rank" (Montagu 1993:137). This episode marks the end of Montagu's ample, and ultimately well-informed, praise of Turkish Muslim women, as well as Ottoman culture more generally. Subsequent letters record her return trip through the Mediterranean, where she was much less generous in her observations of tattooed Tunisian women, who were also relatively darker-skinned than the elite Turkish women Montagu praised. Nevertheless,

---

[26] Montagu frequently donned the traditional veil while in the Ottoman Empire (1993:71, 92, 95, 126–27). She felt this "Turkish habit [or mode of apparel]" gave Muslim women "more liberty than we have" (Montagu 1993:69, 71).

in taking the Turkish Embassy Letters as a whole, we see that Montagu's commitment to learning the Turkish language, conversing with Muslim men and women, and investigating insofar as she could the Islamic religion resulted by the end of her Ottoman sojourn in a document refuting the central fallacies that still compromise Christian–Muslim dialogue today.

Lessons from a Cross-Cultural Dialogue Across the Centuries

Fethullah Gülen's gloss on Lady Mary Wortley Montagu, who is not well known by even educated English readers today, attests to the depth of his commitment to interfaith and intercultural dialogue. The issues raised in this analysis of Gülen's assessment of women's rights from an Islamic perspective and Montagu's developing understanding of Muslim women's relatively higher status than the English women of her era are therefore methodological as well as historical. For instance, while Christians, who traditionally reject Islam as coming after their revealed books, remain ignorant of the status of women as specified in the Qur'an, Muslims may also remain ignorant of aspects of Christianity beyond the Gospels. My explication of the Christian view of veiling, which is specified in the Pauline letters, as distinct from the Qur'anic view exemplifies this need to seek accurate knowledge of each other's religious traditions.

For Montagu, her developing understanding revealed to her the limits of the Judeo-Christian tradition for achieving gender justice. Though women and men in England throughout the seventeenth century attempted to employ scriptural exegesis to argue for women's spiritual and social equality, this effort had exhausted itself by Montagu's era in the absence of any clear articulation of women's rights in the generally accepted Christian canon (Andrea 2007). At the close of the seventeenth century, Mary Astell, considered the first English feminist in the sense she articulated a discourse of rights, had to turn to the nascent liberal political theory of John Locke to advance the cause of women, even though she was a profoundly religious woman (Perry 1986:8–9). Montagu, who admired Astell so much she asked her to prepare a preface for the Turkish Embassy Letters, turned to the Enlightenment doctrine of deism, which rejected revealed religion altogether. Had she been able to remain in the Ottoman Empire, she might have followed other paths, as did the woman in the last episode Montagu records of her Turkish sojourn. Reading Fethullah Gülen's assessment of women's rights from a Qur'anic perspective puts this option into focus.

Fethullah Gülen and Sufism:
A Historical Perspective

Mustafa Gökçek

Fethullah Gülen has attracted attention through the activities of a movement inspired by his ideas and vision mainly in education and interfaith dialogue. The media institutions established by people sympathetic to the movement have helped publicize his views and make the movement more publicly visible. The secular and modern education model established by the participants of the Gülen movement is intended to promote and exemplify cultural tolerance and moral values in role-model teachers, interfaith and intercultural dialogue activities. These activities are aimed at establishing connections among various cultural and religious communities emphasizing tolerance, peaceful coexistence and religious broadmindedness. Gülen has led the movement by designing and proposing new areas of action as well as persistently revitalizing Islamic consciousness and spirituality in the daily and personal lives of participants and presenting an understanding of Islam which is practicable in the contemporary world. While the political and social implications of the activities of the Gülen community have been dealt with in various scholarly works, the religious aspect of Gülen and his community still needs to be analyzed.

In order to fully comprehend Gülen's religious philosophy and the actions of his community it is important to examine the impact of Sufism on Gülen's views. It is not in the scope of this paper to offer a specific definition for Sufism (*tasawwuf*), or to comprehensively analyze Gülen's thought and his community. Neither have we enough space to discuss to the fullest extent Gülen's stance on various issues within Sufism. This article is a first step in a search for the intellectual roots of Gülen's Sufism both in his life and in the Sufi tradition. An analysis of the factors that shape Gülen's Sufi understanding necessitates looking at Gülen's personal background. A review of his Sufi masterpiece *Kalbin Zümrüt Tepeleri* (published in English as *Key Concepts in the Practice of Sufism 1, 2* and *3*) is essential for a chronological and comparative analysis of his views and to locate Gülen in context within the history of Sufism.

Gülen is primarily a scholar, who, while far from establishing a Sufi order, aims to revive and combine the activism of Prophet Muhammad and his companions, the asceticism of the first generation Sufis, and the Sufi terminological knowledge and consciousness of the later Sufi scholars. At a time when the gap between Sufis and their major critique, the *salafis*[1] is increasing, Gülen's main goal is to reestablish Sufism on the basis of the Qur'an and Sunna. Gülen's most significant contribution to Sufi literature is his emphasis on religious activism. In Gülen's Sufi approach the passivism, asceticism and exclusive focus on the inner world under the guidance of the sheikh in many of the early Sufi works are replaced with purification of the self through continuous struggle and action within the community under the direct guidance of the Qur'an and Sunna. This approach offers a new equilibrium within the Muslim world and promotes a peaceful and tolerant understanding of Muslims coexisting peacefully with the non-Muslim communities.

Sufi Influences in Gülen's Early Life

An interview of Gülen published as "Küçük Dünyam" ("My Little World") (Erdoğan 1995) provides many examples of the powerful influence of Sufism on Gülen during his very early childhood. This should not be surprising considering the first Muslim presence in Anatolia was the Sufi dervishes of Central Asia and that Sufi orders have always been influential in Asia Minor. This is especially so in Erzurum, the birthplace of Gülen, which is known for its conservative and spiritual social atmosphere.

---

[1] A school of thought in the Muslim world that claims to focus strictly on reviving Islam as it was practiced by Prophet Muhammad and the three following generations of Muslims. For Salafis all practices other than their own are innovations and thus deviations from Islam.

According to Gülen, the leading authority figure in his family was his great grandfather, Molla Ahmed (Erdoğan 1995:15-18). The qualities which make him venerable in Gülen's memory are all Sufi attributes: asceticism, combining knowledge and piety, living on a few olives a day throughout his life, never sleeping in bed, and sleeping very little. Gülen also mentions his strong attachment to his grandfather, Şamil. He reveres him for not compromising on even the smallest secondary or tertiary aspects of the practice of Islam, respecting the true scholars, and his seriousness. He also emphasizes the influence of his grandmother's spirituality. Gülen mentions his father with deep respect as having a major influence on him and recalls his father's passion for knowledge, love of the companions of the Prophet, and refined manners.

While these instances indicate the reverence for Sufi qualities in Gülen's family, a local Sufi sheikh Mehmed Lütfi or Alvarlı Efe, as known by the locals, was the greatest influence on Gülen in terms of establishing Sufi qualities in his life (Erdogan 1995:27–29). Lütfi paid frequent visits to their house and was highly respected in the family. Gülen memorized the poems that Lütfi recited in his sermons and many of his teachings have remained strong in Gülen's memory, as they are reflected in Gülen's later teachings. Lütfi passed away when Gülen was sixteen. Certainly his experiences in Sufi lodges (*tekye*) in this period of his life left a deep impression on Gülen and this impact is reflected in his thinking. He argues that a perfect community combines three characteristics in itself: the discipline of the army, the knowledge of the school, and the manners of those who learn in the presence of Sufi masters.[2]

The Stages of the Spiritual Journey

Gülen describes the steps that lead the seeker (*murid*) to the right path, or the perfected human being (*Insan-i Kamil*), in his two-volume work entitled *Kalbin Zümrüt Tepeleri* (*Key Concepts in the Practice of Sufism*). In the second volume of this work, the chapter "*Sayr-u Suluk*" ("Journeying and Initiation") describes the stages of spiritual journey such as *sayr ilallah* (journeying to God), *sayr fillah* (journeying in God), *sayr maallah* (journeying with God), *sayr anillah*

---

2 Fethullah Gülen, "Askerlik Çok Önemlidir," Kirik Testi (October 25, 2003), http://www.herkul.org/kiriktesti/index.php?article_id=64 (accessed September 2, 2005).

(journeying from God), and several stages of improving the Self (*nafs*) in the classical Sufi understanding (Gülen 2001:255-273, 2004c:244-262):

> In the language of Sufism, when used together, sayr u suluk (journeying and initiation) denotes becoming free of bodily and animal appetites to a certain extent within the framework of certain principles, searching for ways to reach God and traveling toward Him by the heart in order to lead a life at the level of the spirit and the heart.

Later, under the title "Another Line in *Sayr-u Suluk*" he examines and evaluates the approach of Said Nursi. Nursi's most explicit explanation of this aspect is described in the Addendum of the Twenty-sixth Word in *The Words* collection:

> The ways leading to Almighty God are truly numerous. While all true ways are taken from the Qur'an, some are shorter, safer, and more general than others. Of these ways taken from the Qur'an is that of impotence, poverty, compassion, and reflection, from which, with my defective understanding, I have benefited.
> [Nursi 2001:221]

Besides these four steps, Nursi presents a slightly different list in the Fourth Letter of *The Letters* collection: "On the way of impotence four things are necessary: absolute poverty, absolute impotence, absolute thanks, and absolute ardor, my friend" (Nursi 2001:354). Gülen brings these two formulations together and lists six essentials of this alternate path: impotence, poverty, compassion, reflection, ardor, and thanks. He praises this way as "the reflection of the truth of Prophethood and flourishing of the path of the Companions" (Gülen 2001:288).

Nursi did not write out his thoughts on Sufism and Sufi terminology in a separate book. He occasionally makes references to these issues and offers his own position on certain aspects of Sufism. The teachings of *Risale-i Nur* constitute a part of Gülen's "subconscious attainment."[3] Gülen adopts Nursi's ideas on Sufism and re-evaluates the traditional Sufi literature through Nursi's perspective. Gülen takes up where Nursi left off and takes his

---

3 In Turkish "şuuraltı müktesebatı." Gülen used this concept in his interview with Mehmet Gundem published in the daily *Milliyet*. It means the *Risale-i Nur* has quite a strong influence on Gülen's educational and intellectual background. Thus, Gülen may employ ideas from *Risale-i Nur* unintentionally.

teachings a step further by educating his audience in Sufism as a discipline. Gülen follows the example of the earlier Sufi scholars in defining and describing each concept in the terminology of Sufism. Thus, while Gülen does not deviate from the line of Nursi, his writings on Sufi terminology are definitely distinctive.

Situating Gülen in the History of Sufi Thought

The historical development of Sufism can be divided into periods in many ways. A common way of dividing the historical development of Sufism is as follows: (1) the Age of Happiness (the time of the Prophet and His companions), (2) the period of asceticism, period of *tasawwuf*[4], (3) the period of "unity of Being," (4) the period of *tariqa* (orders), and (5) today (Mustafa Kara 1985:77). While in the period of asceticism, the terminology of Sufism was not fully formulated, during the *tasawwuf* period, Sufi scholars described their understanding of Sufism, and explained certain concepts and terminology of Sufism. Biographies of major Sufi scholars of the early period were also compiled. Thus, while in the period of asceticism Sufis strived to live out and refresh the mystical aspect of Islam, in the period of *tasawwuf* scholars started also to speak about Sufism. They handled Sufism as a separate discipline, just like *fiqh* (jurisprudence) or *hadith* (tradition), with its own rules, methodology, and terminology. These scholars had followers and students, but they did not institutionalize their approaches in the form of orders; those were established after the twelfth century. Sufi scholars of the *tasawwuf* period critically analyzed and reshaped the fundamentals of Sufism, while in the period of orders, in most cases, imitation prevailed over critical thinking in a strictly structured master–disciple mystical relationship.

The Sufi scholars that Gülen follows in his *Kalbin Zümrüt Tepeleri* (*Key Concepts in the Practice of Sufism*) mostly belong to the period of *tasawwuf*. A close study of Gülen's views reveals strong parallels between his approach and the views of leading scholars such as Qushayri, Muhasibi, Tusi, Kelebazi, Abu Talib Makki, Hujwiri, Ghazali, and Ibn'ul Qayyim al-Jawziyya. A common characteristic of these scholars is that they all strive to bring together Sufism and Islamic law. In their works, on the one hand they

---

4 I intentionally do not translate the term *tasawwuf* here to avoid confusion with the generic usage of the term Sufism.

criticize the practices which are outside the law that start to emerge within Sufi circles, and on the other hand, they try to defend the basic tenets of Sufism by referring to the Qur'an and Sunna.

Gülen follows the tradition of these scholars in describing and re-evaluating the terms of Sufism. While he does not create new meanings and concepts, he reassesses the Sufi terminology to present a practical approach for modern-day Muslims. He endeavors to refresh their spirituality. His aim in writing *Kalbin Zümrüt Tepeleri* (*Key Concepts in the Practice of Sufism*) is "to raise the believers to the level of the heart and the spirit." He establishes a connection between Said Nursi's line of strict adherence to the Qur'an and the line of the earlier scholars of the *tasawwuf* period. Thus, I argue that by following Nursi and this group of earlier Sufi scholars, Gülen endeavors to promote a Sufi approach in strict accordance with the Qur'an and Sunna. This emphasis on the Qur'an and Hadith as the basis of Sufism conveniently protects his approach against criticisms of Sufism.

The Formulation of Gülen's Sufi Approach

How, then, did Gülen develop his Sufi worldview? When did he start talking about Sufism? Although Sufism has always played a significant role in Gülen's thought, he did not write about it until the early 1990s. In the 1970s, the focus of his sermons was mostly the basic concepts of faith and Islam, such as the oneness of God, Prophethood and the life of Prophet Muhammad, prayers, fasting, and son on. He did not treat Sufism as a distinct discipline, but the content of his sermons included examples from the lives of earlier ascetics. Sufi conceptualization became much more noticeable when his sermons resumed in 1986. In these sermons, which lasted until 1992, Gülen focused on the spiritual characteristics that an ideal Muslim community should have. The themes were more spiritual: love of God and his Prophet, the aspects of the spirit and the heart, piety, hope and despair, sacred sorrow, the culture of conscience, and so on.

The Gülen community's monthly magazine *Sızıntı* did not include any articles focused on Sufism until October 1990 when Gülen wrote the first of a series of articles under the general title of "Kalbin Zümrüt Tepeleri" ("On the Emerald Hills of the Heart"). These articles were and are still published in the middle pages of the magazine on a higher quality paper and with an attractive design that distinguishes them from the rest of the magazine. When these articles make up a large enough number the community's press house publishes them under the title *Kalbin Zümrüt Tepeleri (Key Concepts in the Practice of Sufism)*. Since October 1990, every month Gülen has focused on a different concept in Sufi terminology. In these articles he usually commences with a generic definition of a concept and explains its meaning in Sufism. He always lists the relevant Qur'anic verses and sayings of the Prophet. Then, he discusses various interpretations of the concept by different Sufi scholars, and elaborates on different stages or aspects of it. Gülen enriches his articles with couplets from famous Sufi poets, most frequently from Rumi, Mehmed Lütfi, and Yunus Emre. Where possible, he concludes his articles with a message to contemporary Muslims and describes how the concept should be understood and practiced in daily life.

In his writings on Sufi concepts, Gulen does not create fundamentally new approaches, nor does he bring new definitions to concepts already discussed in detail by earlier Sufi scholars. Rather, Gülen draws on certain scholars to present a reasonable and practical Sufi way to his readers. Thus, I deem it significant to understand Gülen's choices of views and the earlier scholars to whom he refers most often. Therefore, I will focus on selected concepts of Sufism and endeavor to illustrate Gülen's stance within Sufism.

Gülen and Earlier Scholars on Key Concepts of Sufism

Hal (state) and *Makam* (station) are two key concepts that Sufi scholars utilize in explaining various other concepts of Sufism. One of Gülen's first articles on Sufism in *Sızıntı* was on *state* and *station*. In this short piece he describes *state* and compares it with *station* to present how they are understood within Sufism. These spiritual states and stations are persistently dealt with by all Sufi treatises because of "the fundamental significance of the knowledge of spiritual states for anyone who aspires to pass through them and beyond them to the Divine Presence" (Nasr 1972:68). On this fundamental issue Gülen's approach is in line with the classical descriptions made by earlier authorities of Sufism. For Gülen, the *state* is the disciple's experience and consciousness of the divine feelings that appear in the heart beyond his will, and *station* is the continuity and stability of these feelings through the disciple's efforts and striving (Gülen 2003b:20–21). Thus state is a gift from

171

God, while station is gained by the will of the disciple. This definition is very much in line with Qushayri's description of *state* in his famous *Risale*: "States are gifts of God while stations are gained by effort. States are from God's generosity, but stations take place with efforts and striving" (Kuseyri 1978:150). Hujwiri too, in his *Kashf Al-Mahjub* (*Unveiling of the Veiled*), one of the earliest Sufi treatises, defines these two terms in a similar way: "while the term *station* denotes the way of the seeker, and his progress in the field of exertion, ...the term *state* denotes the favor and grace which God bestows upon the heart of His servant."[5] Thus on the issue of state and station Gülen follows the mainstream Sufi position.

Another issue which is a dividing line among Sufi scholars is *sekr* (mystical intoxication, drunkenness) and *sahv* (mystical sobriety). Gülen explains that in Sufi terminology intoxication is when the wayfarer loses himself in ecstasy upon experiencing divine rays. On the other hand, sobriety is the wayfarer's coming back to his or her senses from the state of intoxication. Gülen calls intoxication a "station," thus it cannot be reached by the will of wayfarer, but it is only a bounty of God, while sobriety is a "state" in which the wayfarer strives to stay. Gülen argues that sobriety should be preferred to intoxication, which is not a path as stable and healthy as sobriety (Gülen 2004c:125–131). Preferring intoxication or sobriety has been a major dividing line among Sufis. Bayezid Bistami and his students favored intoxication because it eliminates human attributes, while Junayd of Baghdad and his students considered sobriety as a higher and preferable state. Although Gülen prefers sobriety, he does not criticize being in the station of intoxication. In fact he defends this station against those who argue that it is venerating a concept which is denounced by Islam. Gülen argues that it is an inevitable station which is not controlled by the wayfarer but a gift of God. Therefore, Gülen is tolerant towards *shathiyyat* (theopathic locutions) (Schimmel 1975), in which the mystic utters words that are exoterically against the law, such as Hallaj's "I am the Truth (God)" or Bayazid's "Praise be to Me!" For Gülen, the person in a state of mystical ecstasy can only be prevented from such lapses by prophetic foresight and will. Otherwise, it is natural that the Sufi might overflow at times when he is intoxicated with the rays of divine love. He also mentions that such mistaken utterances should

---

5 Al-Hujviri, *Kashf Al-Mahjub* (Lahore: Islamic Book Foundation, 1976), 181.

not be taken at face value and should be interpreted within the limits of Qur'an and Sunna.

Gülen shows the same tolerance towards the adherents of unity of Being (wahdat al-wujud). He argues that the idea of unity of Being and utterances relating to it are a consequence of a certain mystical station, of a state of ecstasy, and therefore tolerable. If this thought is formulated in a sober way as a philosophy, and takes the shape of unity of existence (wahdat al-mawjud), then it is unacceptable (Gülen 2004c:171–190).

Characteristics of Gülen's Sufi Approach

Gülen strongly emphasizes the significance of following the Qur'an and the Sunna in understanding and practicing Sufism. In all of his articles he presents Qur'anic verses and Hadith relevant to the topic to support his argument. He stresses taking the Qur'an and Sunna as the only criteria in deciding the reliability of any argument. For him, knowledge of the Qur'an and Sunna is essential for any progress on the Sufi path. He regards the Qur'an as the ultimate guide of the wayfarer in the spiritual realm. Therefore, he prefers sobriety to drunkenness because the wayfarer should be awake in all stations and states to stay away from any deviation from the path of the Qur'an and Sunna. (Gülen 2004c:xix–xx)

Another characteristic of Gülen's approach to Sufism is his tolerance on issues most criticized by other groups of Muslims. In particular, Salafis and Wahhabis criticize Sufism harshly because of apparent deviations from the basic teachings of Islam. The erroneous utterances of Sufis in ecstatic stations are unacceptable for such Muslims. Even Al-Jawziyya, who wrote one the most important treatises on Sufism, harshly criticized the adherents of "unity of Being" and even accused some of them of infidelity (El-Cevziyye 1985:159). Al-Jawziyya was a student of Ibn Taymiyya, who is known as the father of Salafiyya, and thus he did not show any tolerance for any deviation from Qur'anic principles. Gülen, on the other hand, is more lenient towards such errors, but only if they were consequences of mystical ecstasy.

Gülen's most significant contribution to the Sufi literature is his emphasis on action. For Gülen action is as vital as belief and belief can be sustainable only if it is supported with action. Action is an inseparable aspect of Sufism, and contemporary Muslims who are willing to live according to

173

the principles of Sufism should be actively involved in the community, share their experience with others, strive to help others and bring peace to the community. In his article on *Çile* (Suffering), Gülen first describes in detail the approach of earlier Sufi scholars, that is the dervish's period of retirement and abstention from all worldly deeds, and fasting which lasts forty days. In the last section of his article, Gülen adds his own understanding and states:

For those who succeed the Prophets, suffering is, rather than a preoccupation with worship and the recitation of God's Names in seclusion, and the abandonment of an easy life for the sake of torment, the pursuit only of God's good pleasure and approval, always being aware of God's company even while among people, arousing in hearts zeal for worshipping God with sincere Islamic thoughts, feelings and attitudes, representing Islam in daily life in the best way possible, stirring up Islamic feelings in others, and by developing in others the desire to believe. This is the way of the Companions [of the Prophet]. (Gülen 2001:235)

In one of his recent writings, at the end of a detailed discussion of *qabd* and *bast* (strain or spiritual pressure and spiritual expansion or relief) he concludes the issue with the following statement: "Today there is need for people who are sensitive enough to be burnt with the fire that falls anywhere in the world. There is need for people who will feel fire in their hearts about an oppressed child in some forgotten part of the world."[6]

Thus, Gülen does not see a Sufism as the life of an ascetic living in the mountains. Today's ideal Sufis, for Gülen, should live among people and manage to be with God; they should strive in the way of God and at the same time represent Islam in the best way.

To conclude, Gülen's Sufi approach emphasizes the central role of the Qur'an and Sunna, it has a tolerant and non-rigid style, and it emphasizes religious activism. This approach may help other Muslim groups to revise their opinions about Sufism. At the same time this approach re-invigorates dialogue between Muslims and non-Muslims. The Sufi understanding that Gülen promotes enables individuals to rise in spirituality while continuing to be active members of modern social life. Thus, Gülen lives as an ascetic

---

[6] http://www.herkul.org/kiriktesti/index.php?article_id=14 (accessed September 2, 2005)

among people, leads his community to the activism of the Prophet and His companions, and draws the framework of a heightened level of spirituality.

References

Abbott, Nabia. 1998. *Aisha, the beloved of Mohammed.* London: Saqi Books.

Abugideiri, Hibba. 2001. The renewed woman of American Islam: Shifting lenses toward 'gender jihad?' *The Muslim World* 91:1–18.

Abu-Lughod, Lila. 1993. *Writing women's worlds: Bedouin stories.* Berkley and Los Angeles: University of California Press.

Abu-Lughod, Lila., ed. 1998. *Remaking women.* Princeton and Chichester: Princeton University Press.

Agai, Bekim. 2003. The Gülen movement's Islamic ethic of education. In *Turkish Islam and the secular state: The Gülen movement.* M. H. Yavuz and J. L. Esposito, eds. Syracuse: Syracuse University Press.

Ahmed, Leila. 1992. *Women and gender in Islam: Historical roots of a modern debate.* New Haven: Yale University Press.

Aktan, Hamza. 2004. Acts of Terror and Suicide Attacks in the Light of the Qur'an and the Sunna. In *An Islamic perspective: Terror and suicide attacks.* Ergün Çapan, ed. New Jersey: The Light Inc.

Al-Bukhari, Muhammad b. Ismail. 1981. *Sahîh al-Bukhâri.* Istanbul: Cagri yay.

Al-Disuqi, Rasha. 1999. *The resurgent voice of Muslim women.* Lombard: Foundation for Islamic Knowledge.

Al-Hajjaj, Muslim b. 1982. *al-Jami al-Sahih.* Istanbul.

Allport, Gordon. 1965. *Letters from Jenny.* San Diego, New York, and London: Harcourt Brace and Company.

Al-Tabari, Ibn Jarir 1954. *Jami al-bayan an ta'wil ay al-Qur'an.* Egypt.

Al-Tirmidhi, Muhammed b. Isa. 1998. *al-Jami al-Sahih.* Beirut.

Andrea, Bernadette. 2007. *Women and Islam in early modern English literature.* Cambridge: Cambridge University Press.

Andrew, Barbara S., Keller, Jean C., and Schwartzman, Lisa H., eds. 2005. *Feminist interventions in ethics and politics: Feminist ethics and social theory.* Lanham: Rowman and Littlefield Publishers.

Appadurai, Arjun. 1996. *Modernity at large: Cultural dimensions of globalization.* Minneapolis and London: University of Minnesota Press.

Arat, Yasamin. 1997. The project of modernity and women in Turkey. In *Rethinking modernity and national identity in Turkey.* S. Bozdoğan and R. Kasaba, eds. Seattle and London: University of Washington Press.

Arat, Yeşim. 1996. On gender and citizenship in Turkey. *Middle East Report* 189:28–31.

Arat, Zehra F., ed. 1998. *Deconstructing images of "the Turkish woman."* New York: St Martin's Press.

Ashton, Loye. 2005. Defending religious diversity and tolerance in America today: Lessons from Fethullah Gülen. Proceedings from *Islam in the contemporary world: The Fethullah Gülen movement in thought and practice.* Rice University, Houston, TX.

Ataman, Muhittin. 2002. Leadership change: Özal leadership and restructuring in Turkish foreign policy. *Alternatives: Turkish Journal of International Relations* 1(1):120–153. at http://www.alternativesjournal.net/volume1/number1/ataman.pdf as of 10/2/2006 14.18 CT.

Aydüz, Davut. 2004. *Tarih boyunca dinlerarası diyalog.* Istanbul: Işık Yayınları.

Baker, Raymond William. 1997. Invidious comparisons: Realism, postmodern globalism, and centrist Islamic movements in Egypt. In *Political Islam: Revolution, radicalism, or reform.* John L. Esposito, ed. Boulder and London: Lynn Reinner Publishers.

Bandura, Albert. 1994. Self-efficacy. In *Encyclopedia of human behavior,* vol 4. V. S. Ramachaudran, ed. New York: Academic Press.

Barlas, Asma. 2002. *"Believing women" in Islam: Unreading patriarchal interpretations of the Qur'an.* Austin: University of Texas Press.

Barton, Greg. 2005. Progressive Islamic thought, civil society, and the Gülen movement in the national context: Parallels with Indonesia. Proceedings from *Islam in the contemporary world: The Fethullah Gülen movement in thought and practice.* Rice University, Houston, TX.

Berkes, Niyazi. 1998. *The development of secularism in Turkey.* New York: Routledge Press.

Bonner, Arthur. 2004. An Islamic Reformation in Turkey. *Middle East Policy,* Vol. XI, No.1, Spring 2004, pp. 84–97.

Bourdieu, Pierre. 1977. *Outline of a theory of practice.* Richard Nice, trans. Cambridge: Cambridge University Press.

Bozdoğan, Sibel and Kasaba, Resat, eds. 1997. *Rethinking modernity and national identity in Turkey*. Seattle and London: University of Washington Press.

Bulaç, Ali. 2004. Jihad. In *An Islamic perspective: Terror and suicide attacks*. Ergün Çapan, ed. New Jersey: The Light Inc.

Bulaç, Ali. 2005. Fethullah Gülen: An intellectual and religious profile. Proceedings from *Islam in the contemporary world: The Fethullah Gülen movement in thought and practice*. Rice University, Houston, TX.

Castells, Manuel. 2000. *The rise of the network society: The information age*. Malden: Blackwell Publishers.

Çetin, Muhammed. 2005. Mobilization and countermobilization: The Gülen movement in Turkey. Proceedings from *Islam in the contemporary world: The Fethullah Gülen movement in thought and practice*, Rice University, Houston, TX.

Cleveland, William. 2000. *A history of the modern Middle East*. Boulder: Westview Press.

Coles, Robert. L. 2001. Elderly narrative reflections on the contradiction in Turkish village family life after migration of adult children. *Journal of Aging Studies* 15:383–406.

Cooke, Mariam. 2001. *Women claim Islam: Creating Islamic feminism through literature*. New York: Routledge.

Cooke, Miriam and Lawrence, Bruce, eds. 2005. *Muslim networks: From hajj to hip hop*. Chapel Hill: University of Carolina Press.

Çapan, Ergün. 2004. Suicide Attacks and Islam. In *An Islamic perspective: Terror and suicide attacks*. Ergün Çapan, ed. New Jersey: The Light Inc.

de Certeau, Michel. 1984. *The practice of everyday life*. Berkley: University of California Press.

Dowling, Siobhan. 2006. Interview with Integration Expert Sussmuth. *Der Spiegel online*. Electronic document, http://www.spiegel.de, accessed February 2, 2006.

El-Cevziyye, Ibn'ul Kayyum. 1985. *Medaric us-salikin*. Istanbul: Dergah Yayınları.

El-Muhasibi, A. El-Harith bin Asad.1998. *Er-Riaye*. Istanbul: Insan Yayınları.

Engineer, Asghar A. 1992. *The rights of women in Islam*. New York: St. Martin's Press.

Erdoğan, Latif. 1995. *Fethullah Gülen Hocaefendi: Küçük Dünyam*. Istanbul: Ad Yayıncılık.

Ergene, M. Enes. 2004. Introduction. In *Toward a global civilization of love and tolerance*. Fethullah Gülen. New Jersey: The Light Inc.

Ergene, M. Enes. 2006. *Geleneğin modern çağa tanıklığı.* Istanbul: Yeni Akademi Yayınları.

Fetzer, Joel S. and Soper, Christopher J. 2005. *Muslims and the State in Britain, France, and Germany.* Cambridge and New York: Cambridge University Press.

Giddens, Anthony. 2000. *Runaway world.* New York: Routledge Press.

Gilligan, Carol. 1982. *In a different voice: Psychological theory and women's development.* Cambridge: Harvard University Press.

Göle, Nilüfer. 2002. Islam in public: New visibilities and new imaginaries. *Public Culture* 14(1):173–190.

Göle, Nilüfer. 2003. The voluntary adoption of Islamic stigma symbols. *Social Research* 70:809–828.

Grundy, Isobel. 1999. *Lady Mary Wortley Montagu.* Oxford: Oxford University Press.

Gülen, M. Fethullah. 1995. *Prophet Muhammad: The infinite light.* London: Truestar.

Gülen, M. Fethullah. 1998a. *Criteria or lights of the way.* London: Truestar.

Gülen, M. Fethullah. 1998b. *Toward the lost paradise.* Kaynak: Izmir.

Gülen, M. Fethullah. 2000a. *Pearls of wisdom.* Ali Ünal, trans. Fairfax: The Fountain.

Gülen, M. Fethullah. 2000b. *Questions and answers about faith.* Muhammed Selcuk, trans. Fairfax: The Fountain.

Gülen, M. Fethullah. 2000c. *Criteria or lights of the way.* London: Truestar.

Gülen, M. Fethullah. 2001. *Kalbin zümrüt tepeleri,* vol. 2. Istanbul: Nil Yayınları.

Gülen, M. Fethullah. 2003a. *İnsanın özündeki sevgi.* Faruk Tuncer, trans. Istanbul: Da Yay.

Gülen, M. Fethullah. 2003b. *Kirik testi: Askerlik çok önemlidir.* Electronic document, http://www.herkul.org/kiriktesti/index.php?article_id=64, accessed September 2, 2005.

Gülen, M. Fethullah. 2004a. In true Islam, terror does not exist. In *Terror and suicide attaches: An Islamic perspective.* Ergün Çapan, ed. New Jersey: The Light Inc.

Gülen, M. Fethullah. 2004b. *Key concepts in the practice of sufism,* vol. 1. New Jersey: The Light Inc.

Gülen, M. Fethullah. 2004c. *Key concepts in the practice of sufism,* vol. 2. New Jersey: The Light Inc.

Gülen, M. Fethullah. 2004d. *Love and the essence of being human*. Faruk Tuncer, ed. Mehmet Ünal and Nilüfer Korkmaz, trans. Istanbul: Journalist and Writers Foundation Publications.

Gülen, M. Fethullah. 2004e. *Toward a global civilization of love and tolerance*. New Jersey: The Light Inc.

Gülen, M. Fethullah. 2005a. *The messenger of God, Muhammad: An analysis of the Prophet's life*. Ali Ünal, trans. New Jersey: The Light Inc.

Gülen, M. Fethullah. 2005b. *The statue of our souls: Revival in Islamic thought and activism*. Muhammed Cetin, trans. New Jersey: The Light Inc.

Gündem, Mehmet. 2005. *11 Days with Fethullah Gülen: An analysis of a movement with question-and-answers*, Fifth Edition. Istanbul: Alfa; also available in English at http://en.fgulen.com/content/view/1925/14/

Harvey, David. 2003. *The new imperialism*. New York: Oxford University Press.

Hasan, Asma Gull. 2000. *American Muslims: The new generation*. New York: Continuum.

Hermann, Rainer. 2004. *Fethullah Gülen offers antidote for terror*. Frankfurter: Allgemeine.

Hirsch, Marianne, and Keller, Evelyn Fox, eds. 1990. *Conflicts in feminism*. New York: Routledge.

Holcombe, Lee. 1983. *Wives and property: Reform of the married women's property law in nineteenth-century England*. Toronto: University of Toronto Press.

Howard, Douglas A. 2001. *The History of Turkey*. Westport, CT: Greenwood Press.

Huntington, Samuel P. 1997. *The clash of civilizations and the remaking of world order*. New York: Simon and Schuster.

Hunter, Shireen, T. 2002. *Islam, Europe's second religion, the new social, cultural, and political landscape*. Westport and London: Praeger.

Kagitcibasi, Çigdem. 1986. Status of women in Turkey: Cross-cultural perspectives. *International Journal of Middle East Studies* 18:485–499.

Kandiyoti, Deniz. 1998. Some awkward questions on women and modernity in Turkey. In *Remaking women*. L. Abu-Lughod, ed. Princeton and Chichester: Princeton University Press.

Kara, Mustafa. 1985. *Tasavvuf ve tarikatlar tarihi*. Istanbul: Dergah Yayınları.

Karlığa, Bekir. 1998. *Kültürlerarası diyalog sempozyumu*. Istanbul: Erkâm Matbaasi.

Karliağa, Bekir. 2004. Religion, terror, war, and the need for global ethics. In *Terror and suicide attacks: An Islamic perspective.* Ergün Çapan, ed. New Jersey: The Light Inc.

Kepel, Gilles. 2002. *Jihad: The trail of political Islam.* Cambridge: Harvard University Press.

Kepel, Gilles. 2004. *The war for Muslim minds: Islam and the west.* Cambridge: Harvard University Press.

Kiyimba, Abasi. 1998. Islam and science: An overview. In *Knowledge and responsibility: Islamic perspectives on science.* Ali Ünal, ed. Izmir: Kaynak.

Klein, Joan Larsen, ed. 1992. *Daughters, wives and widows: Writings by men about women and marriage in England, 1500-1640.* Urbana: University of Illinois Press.

Kramer, Heintz. 2000. A *changing Turkey: Challenges to Europe and the United States.* Brookings.

Kurtz, Lester R. 2005. Gülen's paradox: Combining, commitment and tolerance. In Islam in Contemporary Turkey: The Contributions of Fethullah Gülen *The Muslim World 95*(3):373–384. Hartford: Blackwell Publishing.

Kuru, Ahmet T. 2003. Fethullah Gülen's Search for a Middle Way Between Modernity and Muslim Tradition. In *Turkish Islam and the secular state: The Gülen movement.* M. H. Yavuz and J. L. Esposito, eds. Syracuse: Syracuse University Press.

Kuru, Ahmet T. 2005. Globalization and diversification of Islamist movements: Three Turkish cases. *Political Science Quarterly* 120(2):253–274.

Kurzman, Charles. 1998. Liberal Islam and its Islamic context. In *Liberal Islam: A sourcebook.* Charles Kurzman, ed. New York: Oxford University Press.

Kuseyri, Abdulkerim. 1978. *Kuseyri Risalesi.* Istanbul: Dergah Yayınları.

Lamphere, Louise., Ragone, Helena, and Zavella, Patricia, eds. 1997. *Situated lives: Gender and culture in everyday life.* New York and London: Routledge.

Lapidus, Ira M. 2001. Between universalism and particularism: The historical bases of Muslim communal, national, and global identities. *Global Networks* 1(1):37–55.

Lerner, Daniel. 1958. *The Passing of Traditional Society.* New York: Free Press.

Lewis, Bernard. 1993. *Islam and the west.* New York: Oxford University Press.

Lubeck, Paul. 2000. The Islamic Revival. In *Global Social Movements.* R. Cohen and S. Rai, eds. London: Athlone Press.

Mamdani, Mahmood. 2002. Good Muslim, bad Muslim: A political perspective on culture and terrorism. *American Anthropologist* 104(3):766–775.

Mamdani, Mahmood. 2004. *Good Muslim, bad Muslim: America, the cold war, and the roots of terror.* New York: Pantheon Books.

Mandaville, Peter. 2001. *Transnational Muslim politics: Reimagining the umma.* New York and London: Routledge Press.

Mardin, Şerif. 1989. *Religion and social change in modern Turkey: The case of Bediüzzaman Said Nursi.* Albany: Suny Press.

McNeill, William H. 1989. *Arnold Toynbee: A Life.* London: Oxford University Press.

Michel, Thomas. 2003. Fethullah Gülen as an Educator. In *Turkish Islam and the secular state: The Gülen movement.* M. H. Yavuz and J. L. Esposito, eds. Syracuse: Syracuse University Press.

Michel, Thomas. 2004. Foreword. In *Towards a Global Civilization of Love and Tolerance.* Fethullah Gülen. New Jersey: The Light Inc.

Michel, Thomas S. J. 2005. Sufism and modernity in the thought of Fethullah Gülen. *The Muslim World* 95(3):341–358.

Mohamed, Sherif Abdel Azeem. 1995. *Women in Islam versus women in the Judaeo-Christian tradition: The myth and the reality.* Electronic document, http://www.islamawareness.net/Women/compwomen.html, accessed June 24, 2005.

Montagu, Mary Wortley. 1993. *Turkish embassy letters.* Jack, Malcolm, ed. Athens: University of Georgia Press.

Morton, F. 1980. *A bibliography of Arnold J. Toynbee.* London: Oxford University Press.

Moussalli, Ahmad S. 1992. *Radical Islamic fundamentalism: The ideological and political discourse of Sayyid Qutb.* Beirut: American University of Beirut.

Moussalli, Ahmad S. 1999. *Moderate and radical Islamic fundamentalism.* Gainesville: University Press of Florida.

Murphy, Caryle. 2005. A Modern, Mystic Ramadan. *Washington Post,* Tuesday, October 4, 2005 B01, http://www.washingtonpost.com/wp-dyn/content/article/2005/10/03/AR2005100301661.html

Nadvi, Syed Suleman. 2003. *Women companions of the Holy Prophet and their sacred lives.* New Delhi: Islamic Book Service.

Nasr, Seyyed Hossein. 1972. *Sufi Essays.* Albany: State University of New York Press.

Nomani, Asra Q. 2005. *Standing alone in Mecca: An American woman's struggle for the soul of Islam.* New York: Harper Collins.

Nokel, Sigrid. *Die Töchter der Gastarbeiter und der Islam.* Bielefeld: Transcript-Bielefeld University.

Nursi, Bediüzzaman Said. 1995. *The letters.* London: Truestar Publishing.

Nursi, Bediüzzaman Said. 2001. *Risale-i Nur Külliyatı.* Istanbul: Sözler Yayıncılık.

Oestreich, Heide. 2004. *Der Kopftuchstreit*, Frankfurt am Main: Brandes and Apsel.

Ong, Aihwa. 1999. *Flexible citizenship: The cultural logics of transnationality.* Durham and London: Duke University Press.

Ortner, Sherry B. 1996. *Making gender: The politics and erotics of culture.* Boston : Beacon Press.

Özdalga, Elisabeth. 2003. Following in the footsteps of Fethullah Gülen: Three women teachers tell their stories. In *Turkish Islam and the secular state: The Gülen movement.* M. H. Yavuz and J. L. Esposito, eds. Syracuse: Syracuse University Press.

Perry, Ruth. 1986. *The celebrated Mary Astell: An early English feminist.* Chicago: University of Chicago Press.

Peters, Francis. E. 1968. *Aristotle and the Arabs: The Aristotelian tradition in Islam.* New York: New York University Press.

Pipes, Daniel. 2002. *In the Path of God: Islam and Political Power.* New Brunswick: Transaction Publishers.

Pope, Hugh. 2005. *Sons of the Conquerors: the Rise of the Turkic World.* New York: Overlook Duckworth

Rahman, Fazlur. 1982. *Islam and modernity.* Chicago: University of Chicago Press.

Rahman, Fazlur. 1999. *Revival and reform in Islam.* Oxford: One World Press.

Rohe, Mathias. 2004. The Legal Treatment of Muslims in Germany. In *The legal treatment of Islamic minorities in Europe.* O. Aluffi and G. Zincone, eds. Peeters: Feiri

Roy, Olivier. 1994. *The failure of political Islam.* Carol Volk, trans. Cambridge: Harvard University Press.

Roy, Olivier. 2004. *Globalized Islam: The search for a new ummah.* New York: Harvard University Press.

Sachedina, Abulaziz. 2001. *The Islamic roots of democratic pluralism a product from the center for strategic and international studies.* New York: Oxford University Press.

Saritoprak, Zeki. 2005. An Islamic approach to peace and nonviolence: A Turkish experience. *The Muslim World* 95(3):413–428.

Saritoprak, Zeki, and Sidney Griffith. 2005. Fethullah Gülen and the people of the book: A voice from Turkey for interfaith dialogue. *The Muslim World* 95:329–340.

Sayyid, Bobby. 2004. *Fundamental fear: Eurocentrism and the emergence of Islamism.* London: Zed Books.

Schiessl, Michaela and Schmidt, Caroling. 2005. Eyes wide shut: An interview with Alice Swartzer. *Der Spiegel online.* Electronic document, http://www.spiegel.de, accessed July 16, 2006.

Schiller, N. G., Basch, L., and Blanc, C.S. 1994. From immigrant to transmigrant: Theorizing transnational migration. *Anthropological Quarterly* 68:48–63.

Schimmel, Annemarie. 1975. *Mystical dimensions of Islam.* Chapel Hill: The University of North Carolina Press.

Schröter, Hiltrud. 2003. *Mohammeds deutsche Tochter.* Ulrike: Helmer Verlag.

Schulze, Reinhardt. 2002. *A modern history of the Islamic world.* New York: NYU Press.

Secor, Anna J. and O'Loughlin, John. 2004. Social and Political Trust in Istanbul and Moscow: A Comparative Analysis of Individual and Neighbourhood Effects. Forthcoming *Transactions, Institute of British Geographers.*

Smith, Margaret. 1997. *Rabi`a Basri: The mystic and her fellow-saints in Islam.* New Delhi: Kitab Bhavan.

Steinberg, Laurence. 1996. *Beyond the classroom: Why school reform has failed and what parents need to do.* New York: Simon and Schuster.

Steinberg, Laurence. 1997. *Beyond the classroom: Why school reform has failed and what parents need to do.* New York: Touchstone.

Stephenson, A. J. 2005. *Making modernity: A Gülen community in Houston, Texas.* Unpublished master's thesis, University of Houston.

Stephenson, Anna J. 2006. Leaving footprints in Houston: Answers to questions on women and the Gülen movement. Proceedings from *Islam in the contemporary world: The Fethullah Gülen movement in thought and practice,* Southern Methodist University, Dallas, TX.

Stiglitz, Joseph E. 2002. *Globalization and its discontents*. New York: W.W. Norton and Co.

Stowasser, Barbara Freyer. 1994. *Women in the Qur'an, traditions, and interpretation*. New York: Oxford University Press.

Stowasser, Barbara Freyer. 2004. The Turks in Germany: From sojourners to citizens. In *Muslims in the west from sojourners to citizens*. Yvonne Yazbeck Haddad, ed. New York: Oxford University Press.

Tages Spiegel. 2006. *Dienstag*. July 25, 19(260):7.

Tahawi. 1996. *Sharh al-maan al-athar*. Beirut: Dar Kutub al-Ilmiyya.

Tekalan, Şerif Ali. 2005. A movement of volunteers. Proceedings from *Islam in the contemporary world: The Fethullah Gülen movement in thought and practice*. Rice University, Houston, TX.

Toynbee, Arnold. 1925. *Survey of International Affairs, 1925: I. The Islamic World Since the Peace Settlement*. London: Oxford University Press.

Toynbee, Arnold. 1934a. *A study of history, vol: 1: Introduction. The geneses of civilizations*. London: Oxford University Press.

Toynbee, Arnold. 1934b. A study of history, *vol: 2: The geneses of civilizations*. London: Oxford University Press.

Toynbee, Arnold. 1934c. *A study of history, vol: 3: The growths of civilizations*. London: Oxford University Press.

Toynbee, Arnold. 1939a. *A study of history, vol: 4. The breakdowns of civilizations*. London: Oxford University Press.

Toynbee, Arnold. 1939b. *A study of history, vol: 5. The disintegrations of civilizations*. London: Oxford University Press.

Toynbee, Arnold. 1939c. *A study of history, vol: 6. The disintegrations of civilizations*. London: Oxford University Press.

Toynbee, Arnold. 1948. Islam, the west and the future. In *Civilization on Trial*. Toynbee, A., ed. London: Oxford University Press.

Toynbee, Arnold. 1954a. *A study of history, vol. 7: Universal states. Universal churches*. London: Oxford University Press.

Toynbee, Arnold. 1954b. *A study of history, vol. 8: Heroic ages. Contacts between civilizations in space*. London: Oxford University Press.

Toynbee, Arnold. 1954c. *A study of history, vol. 9: Contacts between civilizations in time. law and freedom in history. The prospects of the western civilization.* London: Oxford University Press.

Toynbee, Arnold. 1954d. *A study of history, vol. 10: The inspirations of historians. A note on chronology.* London: Oxford University Press.

Toynbee, Arnold. 1961. *A study of history, vol. 12: Reconsiderations.* London: Oxford University Press.

Tuncer, Faruk. 2006. Fethullah Gülen's methodology of interpreting the Qur'an. Proceedings from *Islam in the contemporary world: The Fethullah Gülen movement in thought and practice,* Southern Methodist University, Dallas.

Turam, Berna. 2000. *Between Islam and the state: The politics of engagement.* Doctoral dissertation, McGill University, 2000.

Turgut, Hulusi. 1998. Fethullah Gülen and the Schools: Excerpts from F. Gülen's Answers to Questions on Education and Turkish Educational Activities Abroad, between 15 January and 4 February, *Yeni Yüzyil,* January 27. http://en.fgulen.com/content/view/779/13/

Ünal, Ali, and Williams, Alphonse, eds. 2000. *Fethullah Gülen: Advocate of dialogue.* Fairfax: The Fountain.

Ünal, Ali, ed. 1998. *Knowledge and Responsibility: Islamic Perspectives on Science.* Izmir: Kaynak.

Vandsemb, Berit. H. 1995. The place of narrative in the study of third world migration: The case of spontaneous rural migration in Sri Lanka. *Professional Geographer* 47:411–425.

Viehl, Frauke and Kabak, Sevim. 1999. *Muslimische Frauen in Deutschland erzählen über ihren Glauben.* Gutersloh: Gutersloher Verlagshaus.

Voll, John Obert. 2003. Fethullah Gülen: Transcending modernity in the new Islamic discourse. In *Turkish Islam and the secular state: The Gülen movement.* M. H. Yavuz and J. L. Esposito, eds. Syracuse: Syracuse University Press.

Voll, John Obert. 1997. Relations among Islamist groups. In *Political Islam: Revolution, radicalism, or reform.* John L. Esposito, ed. Boulder: Lynne Reiner Publishers.

Wadud, Amina. 1999. *Qur'an and woman: Rereading the sacred text from a woman's perspective.* New York: Oxford University Press.

Wallerstein, Immanuel. 2000. *The essential wallerstein.* New York: New Press.

Webb, Lynn E. 2000. *Fethullah Gülen: Is there more to him than meets the eye?* Mercury: Izmir.

White, Jenny B. 2002. *Islamist mobilization in Turkey: A study in vernacular politics.* Seattle: University of Washington Press.

Woodhall, Ruth. 2005. Organizing the organization, educating the educators: An examination of Fethullah Gülen's teaching and the membership of the movement. Proceedings from *Islam in the contemporary world: The Fethullah Gülen movement in thought and practice.* Rice University, Houston, TX.

Woodhall, Ruth and Çetin, Muhammed. 2005. Preface. In *The statue of our souls: Revival in Islamic thought and activism.* M. Fethullah Gülen. New Jersey: The Light Inc.

Yavuz, M. Hakan. 2003. *Islamic political identity in Turkey.* New York: Oxford University Press.

Yavuz, M. Hakan. 2003. The Gülen movement: The Turkish puritans. In *Turkish Islam and the secular state: The Gülen movement.* M. H. Yavuz and J. L. Esposito, eds. Syracuse: Syracuse University Press.

Yavuz, M. H., and Esposito, J. L. eds. 2003. *Turkish Islam and the secular state: The Gülen movement.* Syracuse: Syracuse University Press.

Yavuz, M, H and Esposito, John L. 2003. Introduction: Islam in Turkey: Retreat from the secular path. In *Turkish Islam and the secular state: The Gülen movement.* M. H. Yavuz and J. L. Esposito, eds. Syracuse: Syracuse University Press.

Yilmaz, Ihsan. 2003. Ijtihad and tajdid by conduct. In *Turkish Islam and the secular state: The Gülen movement.* M. H. Yavuz and J. L. Esposito, eds. Syracuse: Syracuse University Press.

Yilmaz, Ihsan. 2005. State, law, civil society and Islam in contemporary Turkey. *The Muslim World* 95(3):385–412.

Zald, Mayer N. 1996. Culture, ideology and strategic framing. In *Comparative Perspectives on Social Movements.* D. McAdam, J. D. McCarthy, and M. N. Zald, eds. Cambridge: Cambridge University Press. 261–274.

Zaman. 2006. Turkish Schools, Model for Education in Romania. Friday, February 17, 2006.

Zilfi, Madeline C., ed. 1997. *Women in the Ottoman empire: Middle eastern women in the early modern era.* Leiden, Neth: Brill.

Zubaida, Sami. 1996. Turkish Islam and national identity. *Middle East Report* 10–15.

Index